UNIT E

OCEANOGRAPHY

Theme: Systems

GET READY TO

OBSERVE & QUESTION

What makes up ocean water?

If you jump into a body of water and don't try to swim, will you sink or float? In this unit you'll find out why knowing the properties of water might affect your answer to that question.

EXPERIMENT & HYPOTHESIZE

How does pollution affect the oceans and their resources?

Why is an oil spill such a major problem? Doesn't the oil eventually just get washed away? The activities in this unit will help you answer this and many other questions about the oceans.

INVESTIGATE!

RESEARCH & ANALYZE

As you investigate, learn more from these books.

- ***The Illustrated World of Oceans*** by Susan Wells (Simon & Schuster Books for Young Readers, 1991). Use this book to enter the oceans, the least explored part of Earth's surface.

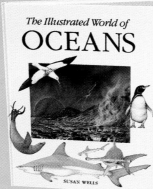

The Illustrated World of OCEANS

SUSAN WELLS

- ***Sharks: The Perfect Predators*** (Silver Burdett Press, 1995). Are we justified in our fear of sharks? Discover the world of sharks and you may be surprised at what you find.

- ***The Black Pearl*** by Scott O'Dell (Dell Publishing, 1967). The oceans hide incredible mysteries that form the basis for many wonderful legends. Enter this world with caution and beware of the monster Manta ray.

WORK TOGETHER & SHARE IDEAS

What would you do if you were asked to market and promote a brand new vacation site— an undersea lodge?

Working together, apply what you have learned about properties of ocean water, organisms living in the oceans, the ocean floor and its features, motions of ocean water, and ocean pollution. Plan and develop the advertising material for this new vacation adventure. Look for the Unit Project Links for ideas on how to develop the advertising campaign.

OCEAN WATER

The waters of the oceans are a vast resource with a rich abundance of life. Yet, the exploration of the oceans has really just begun. What would you like to find out about the ocean waters?

Exploring Down Under

Rose Petrecca says she wanted to learn more about the ocean ever since she watched the television program *Sea Hunt* as a young girl. Now she is a marine biologist and the lead scientist on LEO-15—the Long-Term Ecosystem Observatory. The LEO-15 is one of the world's few underwater laboratories. It is being built off the New Jersey coast in 15 m (49.5 ft) of water. Petrecca and other oceanographers will use the permanent lab to study ocean conditions over a long period of time. Using video cameras and vehicles operated by remote control, the scientists will observe daily life in the ocean. They will check on how pollution is affecting the sea robins, black sea bass, starfish, and surf clams in the water around the LEO. What questions would you ask Rose Petrecca about her work?

Coming Up

▲ Rose Petrecca works on LEO-15.

INVESTIGATION ①

WHAT MAKES UP OCEAN WATER?

You probably know that ocean water is not the same as the water that comes from a faucet in your home. What makes ocean water different from the water you drink each day?

Activity

A Closer Look at Ocean Water

How can you use observations to help you infer what's in ocean water?

Procedure

1. Your teacher will give you a sample of ocean water in a clear glass container. Examine the sample and test for any odor. **Record** your observations in your *Science Notebook*.

2. Use the dropper to place a drop of ocean water on the slide. Place the cover slip over the drop and examine the slide through the microscope. **Record** your observations.

3. Use the dropper to stir the ocean water sample. Then place several dropperfuls of the sample in the clear container. Place the container in sunlight and allow the water to evaporate. **Predict** what you will see as the water evaporates. **Record** your prediction. Then **observe** the container periodically as the water evaporates. **Record** your observations.

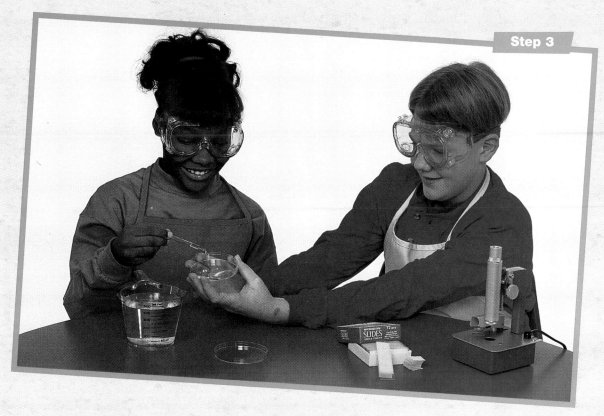

4. When evaporation is complete, use the hand lens to **observe** any material left behind in the container. **Record** your observations.

5. Add tap water to the container and **observe** what happens. **Record** your observations.

Analyze and Conclude

1. **Infer** from your observations what was left behind when the water evaporated. **Explain** your inference.

2. What can you **conclude** about ocean water?

3. Why was evaporation important to the results of this activity?

INVESTIGATE FURTHER!

EXPERIMENT

Predict how your observations would differ if you were using fresh water instead of ocean water. Obtain a sample of fresh water and repeat the activity to check your predictions. Record your data.

What's in the Water?

▲ Water covers two thirds of Earth's surface—from the vast oceans to small mountain streams.

Someday you may have the opportunity to peer from the window of a spacecraft and see Earth floating in space. You'll see a brilliant sphere shining blue, green, brown, and white. But mostly you'll see blue—the blue of Earth's oceans covering two thirds of its surface.

A Salty Story

When you think of the ocean, what characteristic first comes to mind? Do you think of the ocean as being salty? In the activity on pages E6 and E7, you probably inferred that ocean water contains salt and some other substances. But did you know that when the oceans first formed billions of years ago, they weren't salty? Where did the salt come from?

Ocean water is a mixture of the compound water (H_2O) and several salts. The most common salt in ocean water consists of two elements—sodium and chlorine. These two elements are combined as sodium chloride, which you use as table salt.

In nature, sodium chloride, potassium chloride, and magnesium chloride are all salts that are present in rocks and soils. When rainwater flows over the land, it carries away traces of the salts as well as other elements and compounds. The rainwater drains into rivers and streams and then into the ocean. Each year about 364 billion kilograms (400 million tons) of dissolved salts and other substances are washed into the ocean. Some of these substances stay dissolved in the water. Those that don't form sediments, which drift down to and settle on the ocean floor.

Measuring Salt Content

When water evaporates, any solid substance dissolved in the water is left behind. So when ocean water evaporates, sodium chloride and other compounds are left behind. Over billions of years, the concentration of these compounds has built up in the water. On average, 1 kg of ocean water contains 35 g of salts. Thus, 3.5 percent of ocean water is dissolved salts.

The total amount of dissolved salts in ocean water is called **salinity** (sə lin′ə tē). Because the ocean is so huge, its overall salinity changes very slowly. However, salinity does vary in different parts of the ocean. Around the world, the salinity of the oceans and seas can range from 33 to 40 grams per kilogram of water.

Near the equator, heavy rainfalls over the ocean increase the amount of fresh water in the ocean, so salinity tends to be lower there. Areas where rivers empty into the ocean also have lower salinity.

In areas of the ocean where rainfall is low, the salinity of the water is higher than normal, since evaporation leaves salts behind. For example, the Red Sea,

In some parts of the world, such as Great Salt Lake and the Dead Sea, the salt content of water has become so great that salt deposits form along the shore (*left*), and a person doesn't need a flotation device to stay afloat (*bottom*).

which is surrounded by deserts, receives little rainfall. Hot, dry winds speed evaporation. As a result, 1 kg of water from the Red Sea contains about 40 g of salt instead of the average 35 g.

Other Dissolved Substances

Ocean water contains other substances. The graph on page E11 shows these substances and their concentrations. Six substances make up about 99% of the dissolved materials. The amounts of these six main compounds tend to remain the same in ocean water everywhere in the world.

As you can see from the graph, all other compounds and elements make up about 1.0% of the dissolved materials in ocean water. In fact, 80 of the 109 known elements have been found in ocean water. The percentage of the rare elements tends to vary from one region to another, depending upon rainfall, evaporation, and outflow of water from rivers and bays.

Dissolved Gases

Ocean water also contains large amounts of dissolved gases, especially nitrogen, carbon dioxide, and oxygen. (The dissolved oxygen is in addition to the oxygen that is part of the water molecules themselves.) The amounts of these gases in the water depend on many factors, including water depth and temperature. For example, near the surface of the ocean, sunlight helps tiny plantlike organisms in the water grow. As they grow, they release oxygen into the water. As a result, water at or near the surface contains much more oxygen than deeper water does.

Gases dissolve more easily in cold water than in warm water, so water in colder regions of the world contains larger amounts of dissolved gases. Near the equator, the water is warmer so the amount of dissolved gases is less.

Both plants and animals depend on the dissolved gases in ocean water. Tiny

Ocean water is a "soup" of living organisms, such as fish, plants, and kelp (_inset_) along with minerals and dissolved gases. ▼

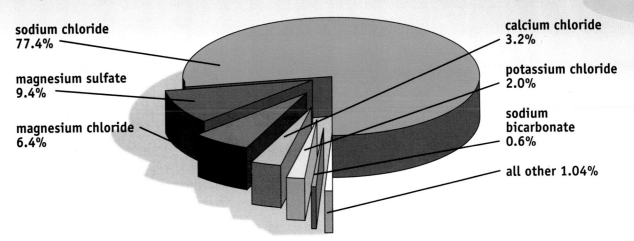

sodium chloride
77.4%

magnesium sulfate
9.4%

magnesium chloride
6.4%

calcium chloride
3.2%

potassium chloride
2.0%

sodium
bicarbonate
0.6%

all other 1.04%

▲ This graph shows the breakdown of substances dissolved in ocean water.

living creatures called **plankton** (plaŋk'tən) float near the surface and drift with the currents. Plantlike plankton, called **phytoplankton** (fīt'ō plaŋk'tən), must have oxygen, carbon dioxide, and certain other dissolved gases and elements to survive. Animal-like plankton, called **zooplankton** (zō'ō plaŋk'tən) feed on the phytoplankton. If a region's water cannot support phytoplankton, the zooplankton cannot survive. If the zooplankton cannot survive, then few other organisms can survive there, either.

Sediments and Pollution

Along with dissolved salts and gases and living plankton, ocean water also contains sediments that have been washed into the ocean or stirred up from the bottom. Sediments might include

sand particles, bits of shells, and decaying organisms. Unlike salts, sediments do not dissolve in the water.

Unfortunately, ocean water also includes some harmful substances put there by people. We already know what human-caused pollution is doing to the water along our coasts. Now wastes from many communities are being dumped at sea and are affecting water quality far out in the ocean.

Ocean water is much more than a mixture of salt and water. It's a complex and constantly changing mixture of water, elements, and living things. This carefully balanced mixture provides oxygen and food, which supports other living things in the ocean. They, in turn, support all the organisms living on the land—including us. ■

INVESTIGATION 1

1. What kinds of materials are found in ocean water?

2. You are given two samples of water and told that one is ocean water and one is water from a lake. Without tasting them, how might you determine which is which?

WHAT ARE THE PROPERTIES OF OCEAN WATER?

All matter, including ocean water, has physical properties. When you first stick your foot in the ocean, what physical property determines if you'll dive right in or run back to shore? What other properties does ocean water have?

Activity
Lighting the Water

Living things depend on sunlight that moves down through the water. How does the amount of available light change with depth?

- -

Procedure

1. In your *Science Notebook*, copy the chart below.

2. Fill a bucket with water. Holding the Secchi disk by its string, lower it 10 cm into the water. **Record** how well you can see the disk.

Water's Depth	Observation
10 cm	
20 cm	
30 cm	

3. Lower the disk by 10-cm intervals and **record** how well you can see the disk at each depth.

4. Pour 50 g of flour into the water. Mix it with the spoon.

5. Lower the Secchi disk into the water until you can no longer see the disk. Grasp the string at the surface of the water and pull the disk out of the water while you hold this spot. Use the meterstick to **measure** the distance between your fingers and the disk. This measurement represents the depth below the water's surface at which you can no longer see the disk. **Record** the depth.

6. **Predict** the depth to which you would be able to see the Secchi disk if you added 100 g more of flour to the water.

7. **Test your prediction** by adding 100 g of flour and repeating steps 4 and 5.

Step 5

Analyze and Conclude

1. **Compare** the visibility of the disk at 10-cm intervals beneath the surface.

2. **Suggest a hypothesis** to explain any change in the visibility of the Secchi disk.

3. What can you **infer** about the available light as depth increases in the ocean?

4. If the water in the bucket models ocean water, **infer** what kinds of particles the flour might represent. How do those particles affect how light penetrates the water?

INVESTIGATE FURTHER!

....

RESEARCH

Work in groups to research the role light plays in determining the color of ocean water. Write a report on your findings.

Activity
Dense Water

Density is a physical property of matter. It can be thought of as how tightly packed the particles are that make up a substance. What factors affect the density of water?

MATERIALS
- waterproof marker
- metric ruler
- plastic straw
- modeling clay
- bottom half of a plastic soda bottle (2 L)
- distilled water
- thermometer
- scissors
- tablespoon
- table salt
- *Science Notebook*

Procedure

	Warm Water	Cold Water	Salt Water
Temperature			
Estimated Length (in cm)			

1. In your *Science Notebook*, copy the chart above.

2. Mark lines at 0.5-cm intervals along the straw.

3. Pack one end of the straw with clay to a length of 3 cm.

4. Half fill the bottle with water. Place the thermometer in the bottle. **Record** the water temperature in your chart.

5. Place the clay-filled end of the straw in the water so that it floats straight up. (You may need to cut off the open end of the straw 0.5 cm at a time until it floats properly.) Use the lines on the straw to **estimate** the length of the straw that is under water. **Record** the length in your chart.

6. Remove the straw. Place the thermometer in the bottle. Place the bottle in an ice bath.

7. When the temperature of the water drops 5° to 10°C, remove the bottle from the ice bath. **Record** the temperature in your

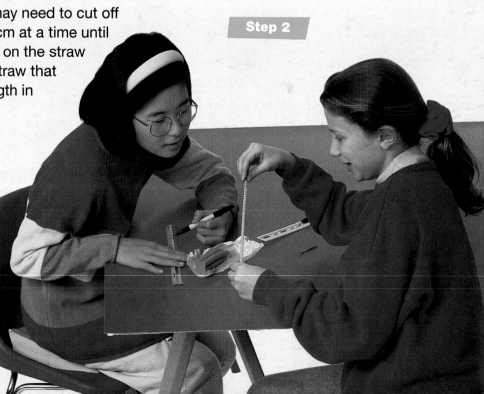

Step 2

chart. **Predict** how much of the straw will be under water in cold water. **Discuss** your prediction with your classmates and explain why you think your prediction will be correct. Repeat step 5.

8. Allow the water to stand until it warms up to the original temperature. **Record** the temperature in your chart and remove the thermometer. Add 3 table-spoons of salt and stir until it dissolves. **Predict** how much of the straw will be under water in salt water. **Discuss** your prediction with your classmates and explain why you think your prediction will be correct. Repeat step 5.

Step 4

Analyze and Conclude

1. The deeper the straw sinks, the less dense the water is. Which was more dense, the warm fresh water, the cold fresh water, or the salt water? How do you know?

2. **Suggest a hypothesis** about how temperature and salinity affect the density of water.

SCIENCE IN LITERATURE

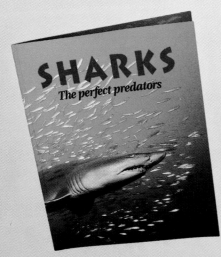

SHARKS:
THE PERFECT PREDATORS
by Howard Hall
Silver Burdett Press, 1995

- Some sharks never stop swimming from the moment they are born to the day they die.

- If you could hook up a single flashlight battery with electrodes 1,000 miles apart, sharks would be able to sense its incredibly weak electrical field.

- Sharks don't particularly like the taste of humans.

These are some of the amazing facts found in *Sharks: The Perfect Predators*. The author, a diver and marine biologist, has been up close with sharks many times as an underwater filmmaker and photographer. Find out how the 350 species of sharks alive today are well suited to life in the ocean.

Activity

Under Pressure

If you've ever dived deep into the water, you may have felt some pain in your ears. What physical property of water causes this effect?

MATERIALS

- pencil
- milk carton
- metric ruler
- small ball of clay
- sink or basin
- water
- *Science Notebook*

Procedure

1. Use a pencil to make a hole in the milk carton about 2 cm from the bottom, as shown in the photo.

2. Plug the hole with clay.

3. From the hole measure up 5 cm, 10 cm, 15 cm, and 20 cm. Make a mark at each point.

4. Carefully pour water into the carton up to the 5-cm mark.

5. Hold the carton over a sink or a basin. Your partner should hold the metric ruler below the hole as shown.

6. Unplug the hole and **measure** how far the water squirts out of the carton. In your *Science Notebook*, **record** your results.

7. Replug the hole and fill the carton to the 10-cm mark. Repeat steps 5 and 6.

8. **Predict** how far the water will squirt if you fill the carton to the 15-cm and 20-cm marks. Test your predictions and **record** your results.

Step 1

Analyze and Conclude

1. When did the water squirt the farthest? Why do you think this happened?

2. Pressure is the amount of force acting on an area. **Infer** from your observations when the water pressure was the greatest in the carton.

3. **Suggest a hypothesis** that relates water pressure and depth.

Steps 5 and 6

The Bends

 People who want to explore the ocean depths need to understand the effects of water pressure. Divers using scuba (**s**elf-**c**ontained **u**nderwater **b**reathing **a**pparatus) equipment receive one to eight weeks of instruction on diving safely. Because of the increasing water pressure, most scuba divers venture to depths of no more than 50 m (165 ft). However, some scuba divers have descended to depths of 90 m (300 ft).

The divers wear air tanks and carry depth gauges to tell them how far down they are and pressure gauges to show how much air they have left in their tanks. Some divers now carry tiny computers that figure out how long they can stay at a certain depth.

When divers descend into the water, their bodies naturally adjust to the increasing water pressure. However, after divers spend some time under greater pressure, nitrogen from their air tanks begins to build up in their body tissues. As the divers begin rising to the surface, the decreasing water pressure can cause the nitrogen to form bubbles in their blood and other tissues. This condition, called the *bends*, can cause problems ranging from itchy skin to brain damage or even death.

▲ Scuba equipment has enabled people to explore shallow ocean depths. Those who go too deep and come up too fast may suffer from the bends.

To avoid the bends, divers must rise slowly to allow the nitrogen to be released safely from their bodies through respiration. A diver who has been at 90 m (300 ft) for two hours may need five or six hours to rise safely to the surface.

To avoid this long delay, divers who intend to explore deep waters sometimes breathe a mixture of oxygen and the gas helium. Helium doesn't dissolve as easily in body tissues as nitrogen, so it doesn't build up quickly and require such a slow return to the surface. ■

Ocean Temperatures and Pressure

January 23, 1960—Western Pacific Ocean: For several hours now, Jacques Piccard and Lieutenant Don Walsh of the U.S. Navy have been descending into the inky blackness of the *Challenger Deep* in the Mariana Trench. Inside the deep-diving vehicle *Trieste* the two men have been monitoring the temperature and pressure of the water surrounding them.

Some time ago, the vehicle passed the 9,090-m (30,000-ft) mark. The *Trieste's* walls creak under the nearly 7 T/in.^{2} of pressure, and the outside water temperature has dropped well below what would be freezing at a normal surface pressure of 14.7 lbs/in.^{2}. *Trieste* stops at a depth of 10,910 m (35,800 ft)—nearly 7 mi beneath the surface. Piccard and Walsh peer out at the cold dark world surrounding them. Strange-looking fish move slowly through the water and a "snowstorm" of sediment drifts down past the *Trieste's* lights as they penetrate the total blackness of the water.

Jan. 23
Trieste is readied for the descent into the trench.

Trieste surfaces and awaits pickup by the mother ship.

On that day in January 1960, Jacques Piccard and Lt. Don Walsh descended into the deepest known part of the ocean. And as you read, most of their descent into the trench was through water that was completely black. Without the lights from the *Trieste*, they would have seen nothing at all. But how can that be? If oceans cover two thirds of Earth's surface, then most of the Sun's light that strikes Earth must fall on ocean water.

Think about the activity on page E12. How did the visibility of the disk change with depth? Visibility worsens with depth because the surface water quickly absorbs much of the light. By the time sunlight penetrates 10 m (33 ft) into the water,

it's no longer bright and shiny. The water has absorbed most of the visible light rays, leaving only a blue-green light. This blue-green light gives the ocean its color.

No sunlight—and no direct heat from sunlight—penetrates deep into the ocean. Although sunlight can heat the water surface near the equator to the bathtub temperature of 30°C (86°F), water temperatures in the deepest regions of the ocean stay near or below 0°C (32°F). Only the tremendous pressures at those depths keep the water from becoming solid ice.

Just as temperatures decrease in the ocean depths, water pressure increases. In the activity on page E16, you saw for yourself how water pressure increases as the water depth increases. Water pressure can be measured in pounds per square inch. At the ocean's surface, air pressure is 14.7 lbs/in.^{2}, but the water pressure is 0 lbs/in.^{2}. At great depths, water pressure can reach more than 14,000 lbs/in.^{2}. Had the *Trieste* not been specially constructed, the water pressure at the bottom of the Mariana Trench would have crushed it, and everything in it, within seconds. ■

INVESTIGATE FURTHER!

EXPERIMENT

Find out what and where the Dead Sea is and what its water is like. Then infer whether its water is more dense or less dense than ocean water. Explain your inference. Also find out why the water in the Dead Sea is the way it is and report your information to the class.

That's Dense!

▲ **If you were to dive below the surface of this water, you would find the water getting colder as you went down.**

When Piccard and Walsh descended into the Mariana Trench, they monitored the increasing pressure and decreasing temperature of the water. They also monitored the water's density. When you did the activity on page E16, you observed firsthand that water pressure increases with depth. However, you could not observe or measure any changes in the density of the water.

But how can water become more or less dense? Generally, as a substance becomes colder, it contracts and becomes more dense. As a substance becomes warmer, it expands and becomes less dense.

As ocean water is warmed, it expands slightly. The same volume of water now has less mass. That makes the warm water on the ocean surface less dense than the colder water at the bottom of the ocean. As the water on the surface cools, it contracts, making it more dense. Then the denser water sinks, while any warmer, less dense water below rises to the surface. Water continues to contract until it reaches a temperature of 4°C (39.2°F). Then something strange happens. Water begins to expand. It continues to expand until its temperature reaches 0°C (32°F). Then it freezes. Think about it. Have you ever seen an ice cube sink? Can you now

As an iceberg melts, it releases less dense fresh water that floats on top of more dense salt water. ▼

explain why an ice cube at 0°C floats in water that is substantially warmer?

However, as you read, water at the very bottom of the ocean reaches temperatures near or below 0°C (32°F). But it doesn't freeze. Why? Actually there are two reasons. First, the water is salty. Salt water freezes at a lower temperature than fresh water. Second, along with the contraction caused by the coldness at the ocean depths, the water molecules there are also slightly squeezed together by the weight of the water above them. This squeezing helps increase the water's density. It also helps prevent the water from freezing even though the temperature is near or below 0°C.

The difference in water density between the surface and the deep ocean is not great. When the *Trieste* descended into the Mariana Trench, Piccard and Walsh discovered that the water there was only 7 percent denser than water at the surface.

However, density is greatly affected by the amount of salt and other substances dissolved in the water. Dissolved substances add mass to a given volume of water. Thus, salty ocean water is more dense than the fresh water in rivers.

When fresh water and salt water meet, the less dense fresh water sometimes floats on top of the more dense salt water. For example, Hudson Bay in Canada is almost completely surrounded by land. At one end it's fed by freshwater rivers. At the other end it connects with the Atlantic Ocean.

In the bay, salinity and density increase as the water depth increases. The surface of the bay has a salinity level of only 2 g/1,000 g of water when the current is strong and the ice is melting, thus adding more fresh water. However, about 25 m (80 ft) down, the water's salinity increases to 31 g/1,000 g of water. Differences in density are an important factor in the development of some kinds of ocean currents. ■

INVESTIGATE FURTHER!

EXPERIMENT

Predict how the results of the activity on page E16 would vary if you repeated the experiment with holes punched at 2 cm, 6 cm, and 10 cm. Try it and explain the results observed.

━━━━━ **INVESTIGATION 2** ━━━━━

1. What are the physical properties of ocean water?

2. What do you think would happen to any organisms found at the bottom of the Mariana Trench if they were brought suddenly to the surface? Explain your answer.

INVESTIGATION 3

WHAT LIVING THINGS ARE IN OCEAN WATER?

The oceans of the world are teeming with life. Some organisms float with the currents; others swim; still others spend their adult lives crawling on or anchored to the bottom. Find out more about living things in the ocean in this investigation.

Activity

Let the Sun Shine

Living things besides humans affect the oceans. Find out one way plants change ocean water in this activity.

- - - - - - - - - - - - - - - - - -

Procedure

1. Place the large jar in an area where it will be exposed to strong sunlight for several hours each day.

2. Fill the large jar with water to within a few centimeters of the top. Roll up your sleeves.

MATERIALS

- goggles
- water
- *Elodea*
- large jar or aquarium
- funnel
- test tube
- paper towels
- *Science Notebook*

SAFETY ///////

Wear goggles. Handle any glass equipment with care. Wipe up any spills immediately.

3. *Elodea* is a freshwater plant that you will use **to model** a marine plant. Place the *Elodea* in the bottom of the aquarium and cover it with the funnel.

4. Completely submerge the jar or test tube in the water. Turn it until it is filled with water. If any air bubbles remain inside, push them out with your finger or a straw. Invert the jar or test tube over the funnel, as shown. Don't let air get into the test tube.

5. After 10 minutes, **observe** and **record** any changes. **Predict** any changes that will occur over 24 hours. **Discuss** with your group any changes you think might occur during that time. Then let the jar sit overnight. The next day, examine the assembly and **record your observations**.

Step 4

Analyze and Conclude

1. Oxygen is produced by organisms that have chlorophyll. What evidence is there that oxygen was produced in this activity?

2. **Make a hypothesis** as to how the oxygen produced by plants affects other ocean life.

Step 5

UNIT PROJECT LINK

Imagine you are promoting a brand-new, undersea nature lodge. Visitors will get to and from the lodge in a deep-diving vehicle used for ocean research. Your presentation will include a moving picture of what visitors will see, a taped narration, and other materials. Begin preparing by researching how organisms are adapted to different ocean depths. For example, you might focus on phosphorescent fish, which glow in the lightless waters of the deep. How might phosphorescence help the fish survive? Collect or draw pictures of some of these fish. Create "storyboards" for your moving picture.

All Creatures Great and Small

Sea Nettle jellyfish

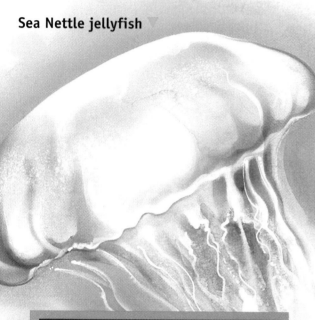

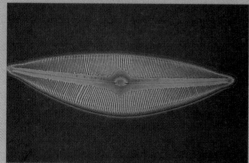

▲ **Phytoplankton and zooplankton make up the very bottom of the ocean food chain.**

Today, more than 200,000 species of plants and animals live in the ocean. These organisms can be divided into three groups—plankton, nekton, and benthos—according to the depth at which they live.

Plankton

Plankton includes organisms that float on or near the surface and drift with the ocean currents. There are two types of plankton, phytoplankton and zooplankton, but there are billions and billions of individual organisms. Although most phytoplankton are too small to see without a microscope, these tiny organisms produce 80 percent of the oxygen on our planet through **photosynthesis** (fōt o-sin′thə sis). Remember that during photosynthesis, organisms containing chlorophyll use the energy in sunlight to produce sugar and oxygen from carbon dioxide and water. The sugar is used for food, and oxygen is used for respiration. Creatures on land and in the ocean could not survive without the oxygen produced by phytoplankton. Because phytoplankton need sunlight for photosynthesis, they must live near the surface of the ocean.

Zooplankton includes some of the young (larval form) of other types of ocean creatures. When they mature, these organisms will no longer be consid-

Common green sea turtle

Nekton includes many varieties of free-swimming organisms like the butterfish (*top*) and red soldier fish (*bottom*).

ered plankton. Instead, they will be lobsters, sea cucumbers, jellyfish, corals, or other organisms.

Nekton

The second main group of organisms, **nekton** (nek′tən), consists of all creatures that swim. It includes invertebrates such as squids and octopuses, all kinds of fish, and mammals such as whales and porpoises. Do you think any plants are considered nekton? Nekton can live at any depth, from near the ocean surface, to the ocean floor. However, each type stays mostly at the ocean depth where the water pressure and other conditions are suitable for its needs.

Benthos

The third group of ocean organisms, the **benthos** (ben′thäs), consists of plants and animals that live on the ocean floor, and do not swim.

The ocean floor starts at the shoreline and goes to the deepest parts of the ocean. Think about the different environments this includes, from waves crashing on the sand to the sea bottom miles beneath the surface. About 98 percent of all the species of ocean life live on the ocean floor. Can you hypothesize why the benthos group contains the greatest variety of ocean life? (Variety is measured

Plants and animals of the benthos (left) live attached to the bottom, while nekton (right) swim freely in the water.

by the number of different species, as opposed to the number of individuals.) Shellfish, such as clams, oysters, and scallops, are members of the benthos group. So are starfish, sea cucumbers, crabs, barnacles, sea anemones, coral and many types of seaweed.

Most members of the benthos group live in shallow water, where food is more plentiful and the water is warmer. You've probably seen cartoons of a big fish about to eat a small fish that is about to eat a smaller fish that is about to eat an insect that is about to eat a plant. This is an example of a food chain. All food chains in the ocean start with phyto-plankton. In one simple food chain, phytoplankton is eaten by krill (a kind of zooplankton that look like tiny shrimp). The krill is then eaten by enormous baleen whales. These whales swim with their mouths open wide, filtering millions of these tiny krill from the water. You've already seen that all creatures need the phytoplankton for oxygen. Additionally, they either eat phytoplankton directly, or they eat another organism that has eaten phytoplankton. ■

INVESTIGATION 3

1. What organisms might you find as part of the plankton, nekton, and benthos groups?

2. Why do you think most plantlike organisms are found in ocean water no deeper than about 9 or 10 m?

REFLECT & EVALUATE

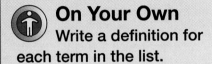
WORD POWER

benthos
nekton
photosynthesis
phytoplankton
plankton
salinity
zooplankton

On Your Own
Write a definition for each term in the list.

With a Partner
Use the terms in the list to make a word-search puzzle. See if your partner can find the hidden terms and tell you what each one means.

BUILD YOUR PORTFOLIO

Using pictures cut from magazines or drawings, make diagrams that show three possible ocean food chains. Label the organisms in your food chains as examples of plankton, benthos, or nekton.

Analyze Information

Study the photographs. Then classify the organisms in each photograph as nekton or benthos. Explain why you classified each organism as you did.

Assess Performance

Design an experiment to find out if salinity affects the freezing temperature of water. After your plan is approved by your teacher, carry out your experiment.

Problem Solving

1. If you had samples of fresh water and ocean water with the same volume, how could you distinguish the samples using only a balance?

2. Give three reasons why a greater number of organisms are likely to live 5 m below the ocean surface than at 1,000 m below the surface.

3. Many chemicals are water pollutants. If a chemical killed all the phytoplankton in the ocean, how would this affect other ocean organisms? How would it affect land organisms?

CHAPTER 2

THE OCEAN FLOOR

Scientists have much to learn about the bottom of the sea,
with its volcanic activity and strange life forms.
There will be many surprises for the explorers who venture there.
How do scientists gather information about the sea floor?

Space-Age Subs

Graham Hawkes is a marine engineer who is busy designing a new type of submersible to explore the ocean. Unlike existing subs, the new submersible will be light and fast. It will twirl and spin, maneuvering like a dolphin. It will seem to fly rather than float to the bottom of the ocean.

The pilot will lie face down, with little room to move, in the 360-cm (12-ft) long body of the sub. The person operating the new craft will look through a clear dome and will steer with joysticks.

The new submersible will be used in a project called *Deep Flight*. One of the goals of this project is to explore the 10.85-km (35,850-ft) deep Mariana Trench in the Pacific Ocean. The challenge for the marine engineer is to produce a vessel that can withstand the tremendous pressure at that depth. Graham Hawkes and his team will make the new submersible out of a ceramic material, which is light and strong. What else do the designers have to consider as they plan and build this new submersible?

Coming Up

Graham Hawkes in his experimental submersible; submersibles such as this will someday explore the deepest parts of the oceans.

WHAT FEATURES AND SEDIMENTS OCCUR ON THE OCEAN FLOOR?

If you were asked to describe the ocean floor, what would you say? For a long time, people thought the ocean floor was shaped like the bottom of a bathtub. In this investigation you'll see how wrong they were!

Activity

Graphing the Ocean Floor

Scientists use sonar to "see" the ocean floor. In this activity you'll make your own ocean floor profile.

MATERIALS
- graph paper
- *Science Notebook*

Procedure

The table provides depth measurements for an area of the ocean off the east coast of the United States. **Graph the data** on a piece of graph paper. The distance from the coast should be along the *x*-axis and the depth to the ocean floor should be on the *y*-axis. Set up the *y*-axis so that the greatest depth is at the bottom of the *y*-axis.

Analyze and Conclude

1. Describe the shape of your graph.

2. What would you call the feature you graphed if it was on land?

3. Infer from your profile how the shape of the ocean floor might be like that of the continents.

Distance from coast (in km)	Depth to the ocean floor (in m)
610	-5988
620	-5840
660	-4965
695	-4520
720	-2333
750	-1895
775	-1754
810	-5110
835	-5840
850	-5842

Activity

Modeling Ocean Sediments

Sediments from the land are constantly being washed into the ocean. Where do they end up?

MATERIALS
- goggles
- 2 plastic soda bottles (1L)
- water
- tablespoon
- sediments of various sizes including clay (powdered), silt, fine sand, coarse sand, and fine gravel
- 2 paper cups
- funnel
- 2 bottle caps
- stack of books
- *Science Notebook*

SAFETY
Wear goggles during this activity. To prevent slipping and falling, immediately mop up any spills.

Procedure

1. Fill the bottles with water to within a few centimeters of the top.

2. Pour several spoonfuls of powdered clay into a paper cup. Add a pinch of silt and fine sand and stir.

3. Pour 2 spoonfuls of each of the sediments into a second paper cup. Stir the mixture.

4. **Model** the washing of clay (soil) into the ocean by using the funnel to slowly pour the clay from the first paper cup into one bottle. Set the bottle to one side and screw on the bottle cap.

5. **Model** the action of sediments that become suspended in ocean water by first tilting the second bottle until the water is within 1 cm of the top. Then use the funnel to pour the cup of mixed sediment into the bottle. Keeping the bottle tilted, screw on the cap and set it aside. Use books to prop it up.

6. **Observe** the bottles for several minutes. In your *Science Notebook* **sketch** the results and **record** your observations. Repeat this step after 1 hour.

Step 4

Analyze and Conclude

1. **Describe** the appearance of the sediments in each bottle after several minutes and after 1 hour. Be sure to **describe** any difference in the way the sediments behaved.

2. **Infer** from your observations what happens to sediments that wash into the ocean.

Features of the Ocean Floor

People build things up and also tear things down. And sometimes nature tears things down for us. Waves wash away sand castles on the beach, for example, and storm waves may wash away homes, boardwalks, and other structures. So it's nice to know that at least the mountains, the rivers, the valleys, and oceans are forever, right? Wrong! Not even Earth's natural features are forever. Its mountains, its rivers, its valleys, and even its mighty oceans have been altered almost continuously since Earth first formed billions of years ago.

Powerful natural forces pull and wrench at Earth's crust, making constant changes. Earthquakes and volcanoes shift huge masses of rocks on the land and in the sea. Rivers carry weathered rock and deposit it in the oceans. So what natural wonders might you find on the ocean bottoms? Are there features similar to those on dry land?

The Continental Shelf

Let's start where the oceans begin. The **continental shelf**, which covers about 5 percent of Earth's surface,

The ocean basin ▼

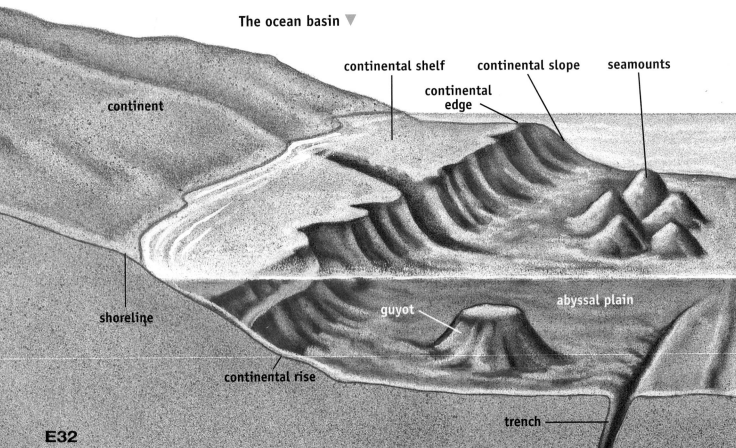

continent

shoreline

continental shelf

continental edge

continental slope

seamounts

continental rise

guyot

abyssal plain

trench

extends in a gentle downward slope from the edges of the continents into the oceans. Throughout the world, when you wade into the ocean, you are walking on the continental shelf. At its deepest it is about 365 m (1,205 ft) below the surface, but its average depth is less than 152 m (500 feet).

Although on average the continental shelf extends less than 80 km (50 mi) from shore, it extends more than 1,120 km (700 mi) off the coast of Siberia. Off the Atlantic coast of North America, the continental shelf extends 144 km (90 mi) out into the ocean. But off the Pacific coast it extends only 29 km (18 mi).

The continental shelf tends to be widest near the mouths of rivers and off coasts that were formed by glaciers during the Ice Ages. Rocks, sediments, and other materials carried into the ocean by rivers and glaciers have greatly increased the size of the continental shelf in those areas.

The Continental Edge and the Continental Slope

The **continental edge** is the point at which the shelf surrounding each continent begins to angle sharply downward toward the ocean depths. The clifflike drop beyond the continental edge is called the **continental slope**. The continental slope is the true boundary between the deep ocean floor and the continents.

To help you remember these first three features, think of them as parts of a gigantic bowl. The continental shelf is the rim (or the lip) of the bowl; the continental edge is the inner edge of the lip; and the continental slope is the inside wall of the bowl, leading down to the bottom like a gigantic bluff.

The Continental Rise

The **continental rise** stretches from the lower portion of the continental slope to the deepest part of the ocean.

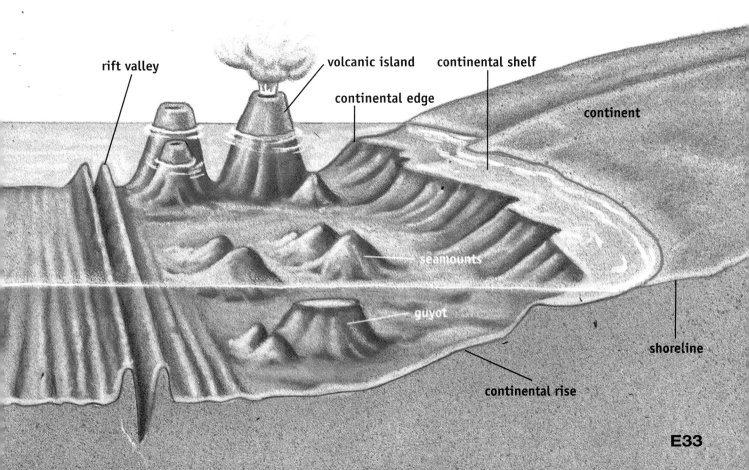

rift valley   volcanic island   continental shelf   continental edge   continent   seamounts   guyot   shoreline   continental rise

Although the continental rise slopes downward, it is not nearly as steep as the continental slope. The continental rise usually begins at 1,425 to 1,970 m (4,700 to 6,500 ft) under the ocean's surface. If you again think of the ocean as a giant bowl, the rise is the softly curving link between the flat bottom and the steep, near-vertical sides.

The Abyssal Plain

Typically, the continental rise flattens out completely at about 3,630 m (12,000 ft), leading into the vast ocean bottom itself. The bottom is called the **abyssal plain** and covers about 46 percent of Earth's surface.

Parts of the abyssal plain are flat, but for the most part, both the continental rise and the abyssal plain feature caves and deep, steep-walled canyons called trenches. Most of these trenches were formed long ago by undersea rivers and currents, and the cooling, contracting, and pulling apart of Earth's rocky crust. Even today the ocean bottom is undergoing change as undersea volcanoes, earthquakes, and powerful deep-water currents continue to alter and reshape the abyssal plain.

Mountains in the Sea

Perhaps the single most startling feature of the abyssal plain is a colossal chain of underwater mountains called the **Mid-Ocean Ridge**. The Mid-Ocean Ridge is the longest mountain range in the world, extending nearly 60,000 km (36,000 mi) and passing through the Atlantic, Indian, and Pacific oceans.

Free-standing mountains, called **seamounts**, formed by volcanoes also exist in the oceans. They are especially numerous in the Pacific, where thousands of seamounts lie beneath the surface. Their tops, which were once above the surface, have been flattened by wave action. A flat-topped seamount is called a guyot (gē′ō).

Covering the ocean floor is a thick layer of sediments that has built up over millions of years. ▼

Some seamounts rise above the surface, forming islands. A spectacular example is Mauna Kea (mou'nə kā'ə), a volcano forming the island of Hawaii. Rising from the ocean floor, Mauna Kea climbs more than 5,144 m (16,877 ft) to the ocean surface. Then it rises an additional 4,649 m (15,253 ft) to a total height of 9,793 m (32,130 ft). It is the tallest mountain in the world, almost 1.0 km (.6 mi) taller than Mount Everest!

So, as you can see, the ocean floor certainly doesn't have a flat, bathtub shape. It is made up of some rather spectacular features. ■

▲ **Would you believe that Mauna Kea, not Mt. Everest, is the tallest mountain in the world? Most of it is underwater.**

SCIENCE IN LITERATURE

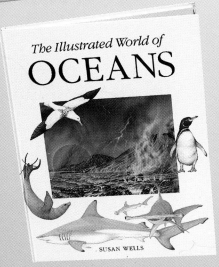

The Illustrated World of
OCEANS
SUSAN WELLS

THE ILLUSTRATED WORLD OF OCEANS
by Susan Wells
Simon and Schuster Books for Young Readers, 1991

- Samples from the ocean floor indicate that some parts of the ocean floor are younger than others.
- Volcanic activity occurs almost constantly along parts of the Mid-Ocean Ridge.

How can the startling features of the ocean floor, such as the Mid-Ocean Ridge, trenches and seamounts be explained? Only by knowing that the crust of the earth is broken into plates that are constantly on the move. Take a look at the shape of the oceans in the past and into the future on pages 16–19 in *The Illustrated World of Oceans*.

You will find the vibrant illustrations throughout this reference book an invitation to browse and become an ocean expert.

Sediments
on the Ocean Floor

Imagine a long, slow snowfall lasting millions of years. Imagine billions and billions of tiny particles drifting down, some so small they can barely be seen, piling on top of each other hour after hour, day after day, year after year, century after century.

If such a snowfall fell on land, it would suffocate the entire world under a massive blanket. After thousands of years the blanket would grow so thick, the weight of the snowflakes on top would crush the ones on the bottom and even compress the rocks and soil underneath until everything sank into the crust.

Sound far-fetched? Not at all, except that the "snowfall" is not snow. It's composed of tiny particles quietly drifting to the ocean bottom. Particles have been settling on the ocean floor since the oceans first formed. Even as you read this sentence, the process continues. The result is a layer of sediments on the ocean floor, forming soft deposits of mud, slime, and decomposed shells that are called ooze. Ooze covers every part of the ocean floor, except where strong currents sweep the bottom bare or where active volcanoes deposit new rock.

Inorganic Sediments

Every time it rains, soil and rock on land are eroded. Some of the particles of soil and rock are washed into the oceans by runoff from the land. Other particles ride the currents of rivers and streams, all of which empty eventually into the oceans.

Other inorganic sediments drifting downward in the oceans include deposits from the thousands of volcanoes rising from the ocean floor. Active volcanoes can contribute great quantities of rock

▲ As this iceberg melts, rocks, soil, and other debris will settle into the ocean as sediments.

Organic Sediments

Organic ooze is found most frequently in the deeper parts of the ocean. Most of the deep-sea ooze is formed from the shells of protists, particularly the remains of single-celled algae. Some ooze is formed from the shells of tiny snails and other small marine animals. Organic ooze covers about half of the ocean floor. It builds up very slowly, from about 1.3 cm (0.5 in.) to about 10.2 cm (4 in.) in a thousand years.

and rock particles each time they erupt. But volcanoes need not be spewing lava and blowing off debris to add to the sediment layer. Constant friction by the ocean currents, plus the dissolving actions of the water itself, continually erodes ocean volcanoes.

Other inorganic particles reach the ocean floor by way of glaciers that fringe the northern and southern parts of the oceans. As glaciers move slowly toward the oceans, they pick up rocks, soil, and organic deposits—the remains of living things. When the glaciers meet the oceans, pieces break off, or calve, to form icebergs. Gradually, materials that were carried by the glacier are released by the melting iceberg and settle to the ocean bottom.

Another source of inorganic sediments is the burning of meteors and comets in the atmosphere. Fragments of iron, nickel, and other debris settle eventually to the ocean bottom.

Where inorganic sediments are plentiful, they form muds and clays of various consistencies and colors. They cover about a quarter of the ocean floor and build up in the thickest layers near the mouths of rivers and streams.

When organisms in the ocean die, their remains settle to the bottom and become part of the organic sediments. ▼

Chemical and Mineral Deposits

During the nineteenth century, people traveling west across the vast plains and imposing mountains of the United States heard it said that "there's gold in them thar hills!" Well, there's gold in "them thar oceans," too. A cubic mile of seawater contains enough gold to make you rich. Unfortunately, extracting the gold costs more than the gold is worth.

As you know, water moving over the land dissolves vast quantities of chemicals and minerals that eventually end up in the oceans. Many minerals, such as gold, are dissolved in sea water. Other minerals build up in the ooze of shallow coastal waters. Although some of the minerals can be mined at a profit, others, like gold and the millions of manganese nodules that litter the ocean floor, aren't yet being reclaimed.

First discovered more than 100 years ago, manganese nodules range in size from 0.5 cm (0.2 in.) to 25 cm (10 in.) across. No one knows for sure how they form, but they appear to grow very slowly from metals dissolved in the water.

Turbidity Currents

Over the open Atlantic basin, the sediment layer is often more than 3,200 m (10,560 ft) thick and millions of years old. Yet it's never more than 303 m (1,000 ft) thick in the Indian and Pacific oceans. The sediment layer also tends to form huge drifts at the bases of mountains and continental slopes.

What causes such differences in the thickness of the sedimentary layer? One possible answer is a **turbidity current** (tʉr bid′i tē kʉr′ənt). These currents, which are still barely understood, seem to occur near the mouths of rivers where heavy sedimentary deposits have built up. In time, the sediments become like layers of unstable snow on hillsides, needing only a slight jolt to send them rolling downhill, like an avalanche. Turbidity currents may cause sediment layers to build up more in some places than in others.

The steep walls of the Hudson canyon were probably carved by the action of turbidity currents. ▽

Reading the Past in Sediments

By studying the layers of ocean sediments, scientists can learn much about the past. For example, one layer of sediments that was deposited at the end of the dinosaur era contains unusual quantities of the rare element iridium.

In some places the iridium level is hundreds of times more concentrated than it should be. Some scientists think that the most likely source for such quantities of iridium would be a single gigantic meteorite or a shower of smaller meteorites striking Earth all at the same time. If a huge meteorite actually did strike our planet millions of years ago, its dust could have blotted out the sun. The darkness would have caused the plants to die, causing the dinosaurs to starve.

The meteorite hypothesis is controversial and may never be accepted by everyone, but it certainly seems possible. It's just about the only workable explanation scientists have for the unusually high levels of iridium that show up in sediment layers of the same age all over the world. It's like finding a person's footprints all over town on a single day. Do the footprints prove the person was everywhere in town on that day? What do you think? ■

▲ **Uh, oh!**

INVESTIGATE FURTHER!

RESEARCH

Water sometimes deposits sediments on land that look very similar to those deposited in the ocean. Do research in geology or earth science books to find out how such deposits form.

INVESTIGATION 1

1. Draw and describe the features of the ocean floor.

2. Why is looking at the sedimentary layers of the ocean floor like looking at a time line?

HOW DO SCIENTISTS STUDY THE OCEAN FLOOR?

You've been assigned to investigate something you can't see, touch, or even get near. How do you investigate something under those conditions? That's the question scientists had to answer when they tried to study the ocean floor. Find out how they do it in this investigation.

Activity
Hear the Distance

You can't see the ocean floor from a ship. But maybe you can "hear" it. Make a model of how scientists "hear" the ocean floor in this activity.

MATERIALS

- timer
- calculator
- meterstick or metric tape measure
- *Science Notebook*

Procedure

1. Work with a partner. Stand about 60 m from a large wall made of brick, cement, or metal. Clap your hands and listen for an echo. If necessary, change your position until you hear an echo. Then mark your location.

2. Clap your hands at a steady rate. Keep practicing until you can time each clap to occur just as an echo reaches you.

3. Have your partner use the timer to determine how long it takes to do 20 of these timed claps. **Record** this data in your *Science Notebook*. Divide this time by 20 to **calculate** the time it takes the sound of one clap to travel from you to the wall and back again. **Record** this data.

Step 1

4. **Measure** the distance between your location and the wall and **record** the data. Then **calculate** the speed of sound, using the following equation:

$$\text{speed of sound} = \frac{2 \times \text{distance to wall}}{\text{time for round trip}}$$

5. Now that you know the speed of sound in air, **plan a method** that uses sound to determine distance. Talk with your partner to plan a method, then tell your plan to your teacher. If he or she approves, try your method at different distances from the wall. Then use the meterstick to check the accuracy of your results. **Record** your data each time.

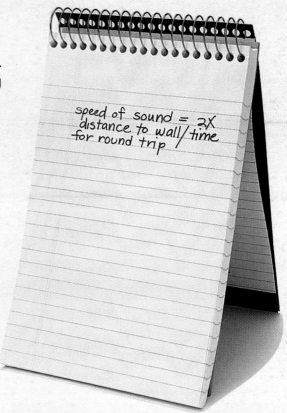

speed of sound = 2 X
distance to wall/time
for round trip

Analyze and Conclude

1. **Infer** how an echo is produced.

2. Sound actually travels through water faster than it does through air. **Hypothesize** how sound might be used to determine the distance from the ocean surface to the ocean floor. **Explain** your hypothesis.

3. How might sound have been used to develop the table you used to graph a profile of the ocean floor in the activity on page E30?

UNIT PROJECT LINK

An important part of your *undersea lodge* promotion is to show where on the ocean floor the lodge would be. At what depth and distance from land would you locate the site, and why? What safety factors would you take into account? Use an ocean map to help you decide where to build. Draw illustrations to show the topography that visitors to the lodge would see. Also, keep gathering data for your taped narration. Remember, your goal is to communicate how unique and interesting an underwater living experience would be.

Activity
Modeling Sonar

Sonar waves are sound waves that can be used to probe the ocean. Find out how scientists collect and use data gathered with sonar.

Procedure

1. Work with a partner. Tie one end of the spring toy to a doorknob and pull the spring so that it is parallel to the floor.

2. Hit the spring sharply with your free hand as close to your other hand as possible. Have your partner **measure** the time it takes the wave motion to travel to the doorknob and back to your hand. **Record** the time in your *Science Notebook*.

3. **Measure** the distance from your hand to the doorknob. **Record** the distance.

4. Repeat step 2 five times and find the average time. To **calculate** the rate of travel, multiply the distance by 2 for the round trip distance and then divide the product by the time. **Record** the rate in your *Science Notebook*.

Analyze and Conclude

1. Sonar waves traveling through ocean water bounce off objects and return. How is your model similar to the way sonar waves behave?

2. Suppose it takes 4 seconds for the wave motion in a spring to make a round trip. **Calculate** the distance traveled.

Step 2

E42

Sonar

Slicing through the water like a living torpedo, a hungry porpoise approaches a school of mackerel. The porpoise follows every movement of the school and soon catches its meal.

Porpoises navigate and track prey by bouncing high-pitched sound pulses off nearby objects. The animal can tell the object's location by the time it takes the sound to return. *Sonar*, meaning "**so**und **na**vigation **r**anging," works on the same principle. The first sonar systems were invented in the 1920s. They were greatly improved during World War II (1939–1945) to help surface ships detect submarines and to help submarines detect surface ships.

After the war, oceanographers adapted sonar techniques to mapping the ocean floor. Modern "side-scan" sonar even works in two directions at once. The system includes a 120-cm (4-ft) metal "fish" with built-in stabilizing fins. The fish is lowered and towed through the water by a ship or a submarine. High-frequency sound pulses go out from the fish and scan the ocean floor. The pulses are also transmitted horizontally through the surrounding water.

The returning sound impulses go to a receiver on the fish itself. Signals then go to a computer on the ship, which prints out visual images on paper. The darkness of the printed image depends on the distance and density of the scanned material. Valleys, rocks, mud, sand, and other underwater features become clearly recognizable. Modern sonar provides a detailed map of the ocean floor that is superior to those obtained in the past. ■

A porpoise's sonar, called *echolocation*, enables the animal to locate and track food.

Underwater Exploration

Explorers have always been fascinated with what could be found beneath the ocean waves. Early in the seventeenth century, inventors began developing diving suits and diving chambers. But it wasn't until the nineteenth century that underwater exploration was really taken seriously. ■

British scientists and the Royal Navy launch HMS *Challenger* on the most ambitious oceanographic voyage to date. At sea for more than three years, the scientists travel more than 112,000 km (70,000 miles), and collect more than 300 deep sea samples.

1872

Matthew Fontaine Maury, a landlubber from Tennessee, joins the U.S. Navy and begins gathering information and developing accurate charts of the world's oceans. He becomes the father of modern oceanography.

1825

Cornelis Drebbel builds the first working submarine. It actually works for a few hours!

1620

1870

Jules Verne's *Twenty Thousand Leagues Under the Sea* revives the ageless dream that safe undersea travel might be possible.

Off Makapu'u Point, Oahu, Hawaii, Sylvia Earle plants the Stars and Stripes at a depth of 378.78 m (1,250 ft), completing the deepest untethered solo dive in history.

1979

1985

Argo, **a complex, advanced underwater survey vehicle, locates the** *Titanic.* *Jason Jr.*, a tiny robot submarine, sends back hundreds of high-quality video and still pictures from inside the wreck.

1968-83

The *Glomar Challenger* **takes up where the HMS** *Challenger* **has left off.** It drills hundreds of deep-water "core samples" from sediment layers all over the world, adding immeasurably to our knowledge of the makeup, age, and natural forces at work in and on Earth.

Exploring the Oceans

Why explore the oceans? Why explore anything for that matter? You might as well ask, "Why eat?" Because, as humans, exploring is something that's in our nature. Soon after we are born, we begin to get curious about our surroundings. So we explore. People have always looked at the oceans and wondered what was under all the water. In recent times people devised some means of finding out.

The first direct observations of what was under all that water began near the end of the nineteenth century. In 1872, the Royal Society of London helped equip the 2,300-ton warship HMS *Challenger* with the most advanced navigating and measuring instruments of the day. During the next three years, the *Challenger* crew sailed about 112,000 km (70,000 miles), measuring ocean depths and collecting deep-sea samples.

What the *Challenger* crew discovered changed the scientific world. In more than 300 locations around the world, the *Challenger* crew dropped a crude dredging device, allowed it to drag along the bottom until it filled with samples, and then hauled it back on deck. A typical drop and retrieval took an entire day. But then, as the dredge was emptied on deck, imagine the scene! Deep into the night, scientists and sailors were still bouncing around on deck, yelling and shaking their heads as they examined by flickering lantern light the day's astonishing finds.

HMS *Challenger* under sail in the Antarctic ▼

A deep-sea lobster brought up by the *Challenger* crew. ▼

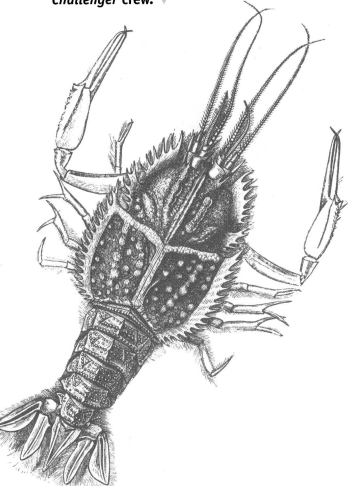

the first *Challenger*. Between 1968 and 1983 this highly advanced exploration ship bored hundreds of holes into the ocean floor and collected long core samples of the sediments. Some of these sediments were 140 million years old. Such core samples gave valuable information about the water, the life it supports, Earth's age, how Earth formed, and the forces that still shape our planet today.

Among many other sophisticated instruments, the *Glomar Challenger* had satellite navigation systems that gave it accurate positioning via on-board computers. In the 1980s, the ship *JOIDES Resolution* took over the job of exploration and continues today. (JOIDES stands for **J**oint **O**ceanographic **I**nstitutions for **D**eep **E**arth **S**ampling.) The *JOIDES Resolution* can probe depths of 8,291 m (27,200 ft), even deeper than the *Glomar Challenger*.

A deep-sea animal-like protist brought up by the *Challenger* crew. ▼

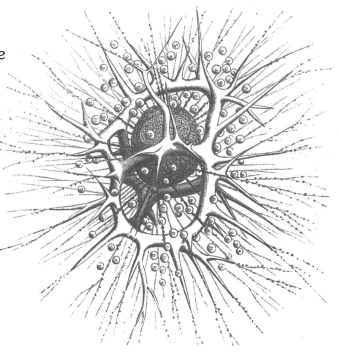

The ocean bottom had been envisioned as empty and barren. Instead, the *Challenger* crew found the ocean to be teeming with life.

The crew of the *Challenger* also took measurements of the ocean depths, using weighted lines. Where they presumed a shallow bottom, the sounding weights fell almost 11.2 km (7 mi) into what became known as the Challenger Deep of the Mariana Trench. At the end of the voyage, the scientists on board the *Challenger* concluded that they had barely begun to explore the oceans.

Almost 100 years later, the *Glomar Challenger* took up the work begun by

Submersibles, Bathyspheres, and Bathyscaphs

Ocean exploration also has been done by some very daring and brave individuals using a wide variety of specialized equipment. The legendary deep-sea divers with their bulky pressure suits, heavy metal helmets, flexible air hoses, and weighted shoes still exist, and are still in demand for specialized tasks. But much of what such divers once did can now be completed by submersibles.

In modern oceanography a submersible is any self-propelled underwater craft. Most are shaped like submarines, though they are usually smaller. They can carry researchers, but often they carry only robots and sampling equipment controlled by computers and cameras.

An older type of submersible is the bathysphere, such as the one used by Charles William Beebe to descend to 923 m (3,028 ft) in 1934. A bathysphere is usually a heavily reinforced, spherical capsule that is attached to a cable that lowers it into the ocean and brings it back to the surface. However, since the late 1950s, bathyspheres have been replaced by bathyscaphs, such as the *Trieste*. Unlike a bathysphere, a bathyscaph is free-moving. It dives and surfaces like a submarine.

◄ In 1934, Charles Beebe entered this bathysphere and descended further into the ocean than anyone had ever gone before.

Underwater Housing

Once humans began to explore the oceans, it was only a matter of time before someone began thinking about living there. In the 1960s *Conshelf I* was built by Jacques Cousteau and placed 10 m (33 ft) deep off the coast of France. *Conshelf I* housed two researchers for seven days. On the floor of the Red Sea at 11 m (36 ft), *Conshelf II* housed five researchers for 30 days. Within your lifetime, researchers and vacationers will probably have the opportunity to spend time on the ocean floor for research and recreation. ■

INVESTIGATION 2

1. Describe some methods that have been used to explore the ocean floor.

2. Using sonar, a scientist aboard ship notes that for the first five pulses the signal takes longer to return each time. For the next five pulses the signal returns faster each time. What is the ship passing over?

REFLECT & EVALUATE

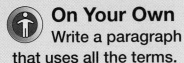

WORD POWER

abyssal plain
continental edge
continental rise
continental shelf
continental slope
Mid-Ocean Ridge
seamount
turbidity current

On Your Own
Write a paragraph that uses all the terms.

With a Partner
Mix up the letters of each term. Give a partner one clue to each term.

BUILD YOUR PORTFOLIO

Imagine you are traveling around the world in a submarine that glides slightly above the ocean floor. Write a short story about your journey that describes at least five features of the ocean floor and some of the organisms you see.

Analyze Information

Study the drawing. Then explain the differences among seamounts, islands, and guyots.

Assess Performance

Make your own core samples. Layer some soil, sand, and clay in different depths in plastic cups. Then carefully push a transparent straw down through the sample. Remove the straw and compare its contents to the layered materials in the cup. Why do scientists find core samples useful?

Problem Solving

1. Sound travels through water at a speed of about 1,531 m per second. If a signal sent from a ship takes 4 seconds to return, how far away is the ocean floor?

2. Give examples of three chemicals or minerals found in ocean water or on the ocean floor. Why do you think many of these substances are not being reclaimed?

3. What advantage do bathyscaphs have over bathyspheres? over human divers?

CHAPTER 3

MOVING OCEAN WATER

The waters of the oceans are constantly in motion. You may have enjoyed watching waves breaking on a beach. While on a boat ride, you may have felt the rhythmic motion of the sea. Yet some waves are powerful enough to alter the course of ships at sea. What do we know about ocean water and how it moves?

Killer Waves

A tsunami (tsσ̄ο nä'mē) is an earthquake-generated wave that races across the ocean at 800 km/h (500 mph). As it travels, it can be thousands of feet deep, extending from the ocean floor to the surface, and it can be hundreds of miles long.

A tsunami slowly builds in size as it approaches land, sometimes to a height of 27 m (90 ft) above sea level. When such a wave hits the shore, it can cause great destruction.

Hiroo Kanamori of Caltech in California is a seismologist (sīz mäl'ə jist), a scientist who deals with earthquakes. He seeks to understand how tsunamis are produced. He believes that mild, hardly noticeable, undersea earthquakes slowly move the ocean floor. An enormous amount of water between the ocean floor and its surface is pushed up. Why do you think this would cause tsunami waves to develop on the ocean surface?

Coming Up

◄ Hiroo Kanamori in his lab at Caltech in California

E51

INVESTIGATION 1

WHAT CAUSES OCEAN CURRENTS?

Thrown overboard by a passenger on a ship, a message in a bottle floats in the ocean for ten years. Then, after being carried thousands of kilometers by ocean currents, it washes onto a lonely shore. How are ocean currents formed?

Activity

Current Trends

A moving stream of air is called wind. In this activity you'll find out how winds and currents are related.

MATERIALS
- goggles
- rectangular pan
- water
- pepper
- straw
- *Science Notebook*

Procedure

1. Wear goggles during this activity. **Record** all observations and responses in your *Science Notebook*.

2. Fill a pan with water to within 1 cm of the top. Sprinkle pepper on the surface of the water.

3. **Predict** what will happen if you gently blow across the surface of the water through a straw. **Record** your prediction in your Science Notebook.

Step 2

4. **Test** your prediction by blowing across the water through a straw. In your *Science Notebook*, **sketch** and **record** your observations.

5. **Predict** what will happen if you blow harder across the surface of the water.

6. Repeat step 4, this time blowing harder.

Analyze and Conclude

1. What did you observe when you blew across the surface of the water?

2. How does a stronger "wind" affect the water?

3. Currents are rivers of water in oceans and other bodies of water. **Suggest a hypothesis** on the role wind plays in producing currents.

INVESTIGATE FURTHER!

RESEARCH

What is the Sargasso Sea and how is it connected to ocean currents? Research and write a report of your findings. Be sure to include any interesting superstitions or tales you discover concerning the Sargasso Sea.

Step 4

Activity

Modeling Density Currents

Recall from Chapter 1 that differences in density cause ocean water to move. In this activity you'll make a model of one kind of density current.

Procedure

1. Pour water into a jar until it is about three-fourths full. Add 1/2 spoonful of salt. Stir the mixture well.

2. Half-fill a cup with water. Add 4 spoonfuls of salt. Add several drops of food coloring and stir the mixture well.

3. **Predict** what will happen if you slowly and carefully pour the contents of the cup into the jar. **Test your prediction.**

4. Wait 2 minutes and **describe** what you observe.

5. **Predict** how the liquid will change in 10 minutes. Let the jar of liquid sit for 10 minutes. Then **describe** what you observe.

Step 2

Analyze and Conclude

1. **Describe** what you observed in steps 4 and 5.

2. Which liquid was more dense? How do you know it was more dense?

3. In this activity you made a model of density currents that move water between the ocean's surface and its depths. Based on your observations, **hypothesize** what causes such currents.

Step 3

World Currents

The ocean is never still. It's restless and constantly moving, and it's a partner of the land and atmosphere in shaping Earth's surface. So how do we begin to talk about the restless oceans? Let's start with the great rivers of water that move through them. These rivers, called **currents**, move water through all parts of the ocean. Some currents, deep under the surface, move very slowly. Others, near the surface, move very quickly.

What Causes Currents?

The speed and direction of surface currents is determined by two factors— the wind and Earth's rotation. Remember what happened on pages E52 and E53 when you blew on the water? Moving air produced moving water. The same thing happens in the ocean. When the wind blows, it pushes water in the direction it is blowing. Although these water movements are called surface currents, the wind affects water under the surface as well. A surface current often carries more water than the largest rivers and travels at speeds ranging from 10 to 160 km (6 to 100 mi) a day.

Since the wind produces surface currents, the direction of the wind affects the direction of ocean currents. Let's look more closely at Earth's winds.

Even from high above Earth's surface, the Gulf Stream shows up as a dark blue river flowing north off the eastern coast of Florida. ▼

Gulfstream

E55

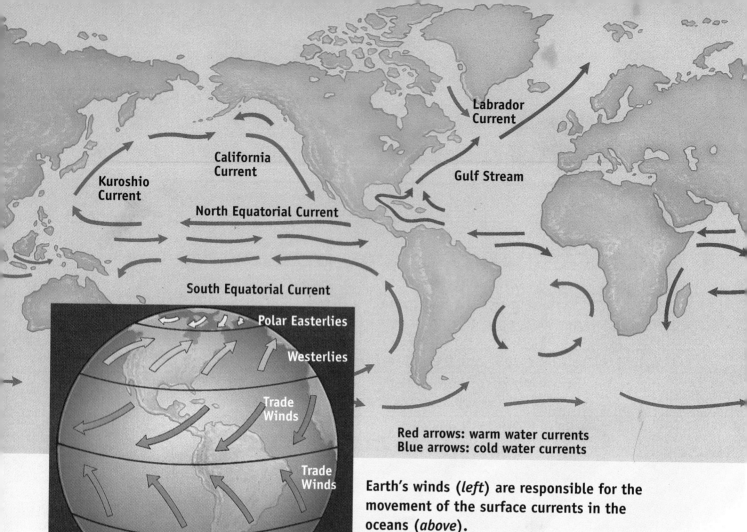

Kuroshio Current

California Current

North Equatorial Current

South Equatorial Current

Labrador Current

Gulf Stream

Polar Easterlies

Westerlies

Trade Winds

Trade Winds

Westerlies

Polar Easterlies

Red arrows: warm water currents
Blue arrows: cold water currents

Earth's winds (*left*) are responsible for the movement of the surface currents in the oceans (*above*).

Examine the diagram of Earth's wind belts. You'll notice that the winds tend to blow across the surface in curved paths rather than in straight lines. In the Northern Hemisphere, Earth's rotation causes the motion of the winds to be bent and shifted in a clockwise direction. In the Southern Hemisphere, Earth's rotation causes the winds to follow counterclockwise paths. The curving motion caused by Earth's rotation is called the **Coriolis effect**. It was named for Gaspard de Coriolis, the French mathematician who explained it.

Some of the winds, called **trade winds**, move from east to west toward the equator. As the trade winds move over the oceans, they push surface currents from east to west. Other winds, called the **westerlies**, blow from west to east, pushing surface currents along with them.

If you examine the two maps above, you will see that the surface ocean currents of the world, like the Gulf Stream and the Kuroshio Current, follow the same general patterns as the global wind belts. The prevailing winds push the water in about the same curving pattern as the wind.

On the maps, notice how the surface currents that begin in warm areas carry warm water, whereas those that begin near the North and South poles carry cold water. How do you think the temperature of ocean currents affect us on land?

How Currents Affect Us

Winds cause currents, and currents influence something that affects us each day—the weather. One current that affects weather in parts of North America and Europe is the Gulf Stream.

The Gulf Stream is one of the Atlantic Ocean's main warm-water surface currents. It moves 100 times more water than all of Earth's rivers combined! The Gulf Stream influences the weather on land by bringing warm water from the equator up the eastern coast of the

United States. This water warms the air, producing weather conditions that are milder than they would be without the Gulf Stream, particularly in winter. Then the Gulf Stream crosses the Atlantic and produces the same effects along Europe's western coast.

When the pattern of ocean currents changes, the weather on land can change, too. One country that is greatly affected by changes in ocean currents is India. Twice a year, India's coastal currents are affected when winds, called monsoons, change direction. When this

happens, the amount of rainfall and the temperature on land also change. The people of India have come to expect this weather change and depend on it for growing their crops.

Large areas of the world are affected by changes in a surface current called El Niño (el nēn'yō). Trade winds blowing across the Pacific Ocean usually keep warm water away from the coasts of North and South America. When these winds weaken, the warm El Niño current reaches these coasts. This current changes position every two to seven years. When it changes position, it causes dramatic changes in the climate, ranging from drought in some areas to frequent storms in others. ■

Although they are at the same latitude above the equator, Dublin, Ireland (*left*) and Newfoundland (*right*) have very different weather because of the Gulf Stream. Both of these pictures were taken at about the same time in winter.

How Deep Water Moves

Did you know that currents deep in the oceans often move in the opposite direction from surface currents? Deep currents also tend to move more slowly than surface currents, traveling from 91 m to 5 km (300 ft to 3 mi) a day. And deep currents are not formed in the same way as surface currents.

You have learned that surface currents are powered by the winds. For the most part, deep ocean currents are driven by differences in water density. Density refers to the mass of a substance compared to the amount of space it takes up. If you have two samples of water that take up the same amount of space, the sample with the greater mass is more dense. Just as dense air sinks in the atmosphere, dense water sinks in the oceans. It's this sinking of dense water that starts deep water currents moving. The density of ocean water depends on three things: salinity, temperature, and sediment content.

Pass the Salt

In Chapter 1 you found that different parts of the ocean contain different amounts of salt. When you did the activity on page E54, you investigated two water samples with different salinities and saw that salt increases the density of water. In fact, the more salt there is in a body of water, the more dense the water becomes.

▲ At the Strait of Gibraltar, less salty water from the Atlantic flows into the Mediterranean Sea above the saltier water that is flowing out into the Atlantic.

For centuries, sailors and scientists watched water flow constantly into the Mediterranean Sea without increasing the water depth. They couldn't figure out where the extra water went. It wasn't until the late 1600s that a deep density current moving from the Mediterranean Sea into the Atlantic Ocean was discovered.

What causes this current? The hot, dry air above the Mediterranean Sea makes surface water evaporate. The surface water that remains becomes saltier and therefore more dense. This dense, salty water sinks and then flows into the Atlantic Ocean. The less salty water in

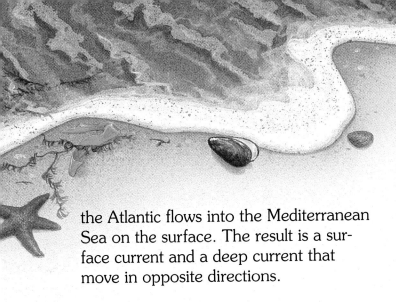

the Atlantic flows into the Mediterranean Sea on the surface. The result is a surface current and a deep current that move in opposite directions.

Running Hot and Cold

If you poured cold water into a tub of warm water, what do you think would happen? Although some mixing occurs, the cold water would tend to sink below the warm water. That's because cold water is more dense than warm water.

Some deep currents begin in the icy-cold waters near the North and South poles. Water near the poles is very dense, in part because it is so cold but also because it is very salty. When water freezes, as it does near the poles, most

of the salt stays behind in the unfrozen water. This dense polar water sinks to the ocean floor and flows under warmer water toward the equator.

Two of these deep currents are shown in the diagram. Notice that the Antarctic Bottom Water flows from the South Pole under the North Atlantic Deep Water, which begins near Greenland. The Antarctic Bottom Water is the coldest, densest water in all the oceans. Some of the water from these deep currents moves slowly toward the equator, warms, and rises slowly toward the surface. Then it begins to flow back toward the pole it came from. However, some of the water stays near the bottom and may circle there for as long as a thousand years!

The area of contact between the Antarctic Bottom Water and the North Atlantic Deep Water is indicated by a light blue wavy boundary. The Antarctic Bottom Water is so cold and dense that most of it is forced to the bottom. However, some of the Antarctic water flows near the surface, warms a little, and flows above the North Atlantic water. ▽

Here in the Antarctic, the coldest, densest water in the oceans sinks to the bottom and begins to flow north. ▽

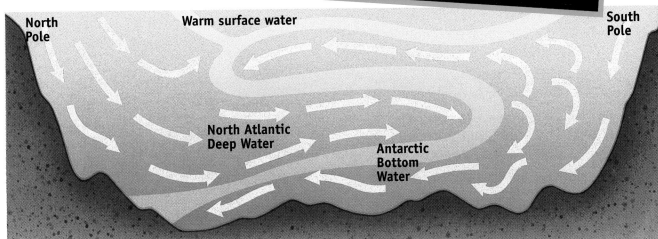

North Pole

Warm surface water

South Pole

North Atlantic Deep Water

Antarctic Bottom Water

Nutrients, such as zooplankton (*inset*), that are brought to the surface by upwelling currents are eaten by some of the world's largest organisms (*above*).

Water From the Depths

In some coastal areas, winds blow surface water away from the shore. This forces deep currents to flow up and replace the surface water. The rising of deep water to the surface is called **upwelling**.

In the ocean, minerals and detritus—bits of shells and dead organisms—constantly drift down to the ocean floor. An upwelling of cold water carries them back up to the surface where they provide phytoplankton and zooplankton with nourishment. The phytoplankton and zooplankton, in turn, nourish many other kinds of ocean life. This is why areas of upwelling often have abundant sea life.

Upwelling is constant in the Antarctic seas, where cooling surface water sinks and is replaced by warmer water from below. Here, upwelling supports a food chain that begins with phytoplankton, zooplankton, and krill. This food chain goes on to include hundreds of thousands of whales, tens of millions of seals, and hundreds of millions of birds.

Off the coasts of Chile and Peru, upwelling supports the fishing industries by bringing up food for fish. But when the warm El Niño current flows in this area, it prevents the normal upwelling of nutrients since upwelling cannot occur where there is warm surface water. The

UNIT PROJECT LINK

During a stay at the undersea lodge, one-day side trips in the deep-diving vehicle will be offered to visitors. Refer to the world map of ocean currents on page E56. Plan a number of trips from the lodge. Take into account how deep-sea currents affect sea life, visibility, and the stability of the vehicle. Where will you go and what will be seen? Make a map of the routes, using pushpins and labels to explain your choices.

◄ Since the ocean has been used as a dumping ground for wastes, it's important to know how currents are going to move those wastes.

zooplankton have nothing to feed on, so they die. Once the zooplankton die, small fish have nothing to feed on. They leave the coast, and the fishing business is affected until the El Niño shifts again.

Dense Sediment

Have you ever dropped a pebble into a pond? If so, you know it sinks to the bottom. Pebbles, sand, and other sediments are denser than water. When sediment mixes with ocean water, it can sink to form a **turbidity current**.

Turbidity currents form when earthquakes or flood waters flowing from rivers into the ocean send large amounts of sediment into the ocean. As the sedi-ment slides down the continental slope toward the ocean floor, it forms an underwater avalanche that can travel up to 80 km/h (50 mph).

As the turbidity current moves, the swirling sediment erodes the ocean floor. According to some scientists, it's possible that turbidity currents actually were responsible for carving out the steep walls of underwater canyons found on the ocean bottom. Unlike other deep currents, turbidity currents are only temporary. After the turbidity current reaches the ocean floor, it slows down, and the sediment settles out.

Scientists study deep currents to learn how they affect surface currents, ocean life, and weather. Since the ocean floor is being considered as a dumping ground for wastes, the more scientists know about deep currents, the better they will be able to predict the possible movement and spread of those wastes. ■

INVESTIGATION 1

THINK IT WRITE IT

1. What role does wind play in creating currents?

2. How are surface currents and deep currents alike? How are they different?

INVESTIGATION 2

WHAT CAUSES OCEAN WAVES?

You sit on a sandy beach and watch the waves crash against the shore. The next day, the surface of the water is calm, and waves gently lap your feet as you walk along the beach. Why does the force of the waves vary from day to day? How are ocean waves formed?

Activity
Making Waves

You saw in Investigation 1 how steadily blowing winds result in the world's ocean currents. Wind can cause another, more familiar movement of surface water.

MATERIALS
- rectangular pan
- water
- cardboard
- metric ruler
- *Science Notebook*

Procedure

1. Fill a pan with water until the water reaches a level 2 cm from the top.

Step 1

2. Hold a piece of cardboard at about a 45° angle to the water's surface. Blow gently down the side of the cardboard. **Record** your observations in your *Science Notebook*.

3. **Predict** what would happen if you blew harder down the side of the cardboard. **Test** your prediction and **record** your observations.

4. **Predict** how the waves will be affected if you blow on the water for a longer period of time. **Test** your prediction and **record** your observations.

Analyze and Conclude

1. How were waves produced?

2. How did the waves vary in steps 2, 3, and 4? What caused the variation?

3. Based on your observations, **hypothesize** how the creation of waves differs from the creation of currents.

4. **Name** two factors that affect the size of ocean waves.

INVESTIGATE FURTHER!

EXPERIMENT

Predict how an island might affect the size of waves. Use a larger or smaller pan and add an "island." Then retry the activity and describe what happens.

Activity
Wave Motion

How do the particles of water move within a wave?

MATERIALS
- goggles
- spring toy
- string
- ribbon
- tape
- meterstick
- *Science Notebook*

SAFETY /////
Wear goggles during this activity.

Procedure

1. With a piece of string, tie one end of a spring toy to a doorknob.

2. Pull the spring so that it is as taut and parallel to the floor as possible. Have your partner tie a short piece of ribbon to one of the loops in the middle of the spring. Mark the position of the ribbon by placing tape on the floor beneath the ribbon. **Measure** the height of the ribbon knot above the floor.

3. Slowly shake the spring up and down to form a wave. Watch the movement of the ribbon as the wave moves along the spring. **Observe** how the ribbon moves relative to the tape. Form waves of different heights to confirm your observations. Each time, have your partner **measure** the height of the wave and **record** your observations in your *Science Notebook* in a chart like the one below. **Sketch** what you observe.

Step 2

Wave Trial	Height	Observations
1		
2		
3		
4		

Analyze and Conclude

1. How did the ribbon move with the wave?

2. **Infer** from your observations how the water particles in a wave move.

3. How did the height of the wave affect the movement of the ribbon?

What Are Waves?

If you've ever jumped into a pool or visited the ocean, you've seen the water's surface move up and down. These up-and-down movements in the ocean are called **waves**.

Measuring Waves

The top of a wave is called the **crest**. A wave's height is the distance from the crest to the level ocean surface. The distance between two successive waves is the **wavelength**. Both height and wavelength can vary for ocean waves.

It is also possible to measure how fast a wave is moving. A **period** is the time it takes for two successive wave crests to pass the same point. The periods for ocean waves usually range from 2 to 20 seconds. This means that the speeds of waves range from 11 to 113 km/h (7 to 70 mph). Most ocean waves travel at about 56 km/h (35 mph).

Movement of Waves

How do the water particles in a wave move? In the activity on page E64, you used a ribbon tied to a spring to model one of these particles. You should have inferred that water particles do not move forward with a wave. Look at the particles represented by circles in the diagram. As the wave passes by, the particles roll in a somersault but end up back where they started. Water particles near the surface turn the biggest somersaults. The motion of the particles decreases as the depth increases.

What controls how big waves get? Think back to when you modeled wind blowing on the ocean on pages E62 and E63. What created the biggest waves?

The harder the wind blows, the higher the waves become. A wind of 48 km/h (30 mph) can cause waves 4.5 m (15 ft) high. The highest wave ever measured

As a wave approaches shore, the wave falls over, or breaks. ▼

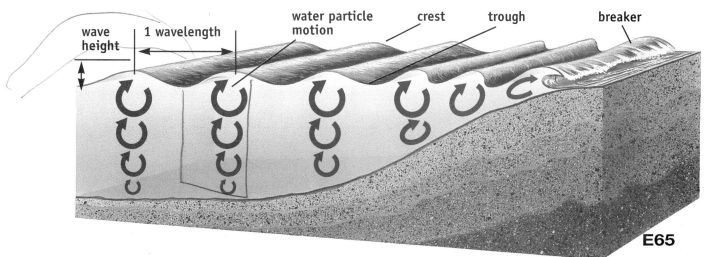

wave height

1 wavelength

water particle motion

crest

trough

breaker

was during a severe storm with winds of more than 88 km/h (55 mph). The wave reached 34 m (112 ft) high, as tall as a ten-story building.

The size of a wave also depends on how long the wind blows and how far it blows. The distance the wind blows over open water is called the **fetch**. The longer the wind blows and the longer the fetch, the bigger the waves become.

When the wind blows hard, the crest of a wave can outrun the lower part. This makes the crest fall forward and break into foam, called a whitecap.

When waves travel from a windy part of the ocean to a calmer area, their crests may become lower and smoother. These waves, called swells, are far apart and can have a wavelength of as much as 1 km (0.6 mi). Swells can travel long dis-

▲ **Wind can generate huge storm waves.**

tances, even passing from one ocean to another since all oceans are connected.

SCIENCE IN LITERATURE

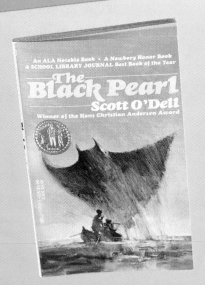

THE BLACK PEARL
by Scott O'Dell
Dell Publishing, 1967

Ramón Salazar, raised with the legend of a monster manta ray that haunts the coastal waters of Baja California, finds a huge pearl of incredible value. *The Black Pearl* is Ramón's story of the events that surround this great fortune. Told with the power of a legend that has been passed from generation to generation, author Scott O'Dell will keep you guessing. What parts of this story could be real? Which parts are more like a dream?

Read the story and share your impressions with others. What does the story tell you about the importance of knowing the ways of the sea to the people of this Mexican village?

▲ **Unless protected, homes near the shoreline are often in danger from storm-generated waves.**

Waves and Land

Waves pick up and deposit sediment. Even gentle waves can combine with surface currents to move huge amounts of sand from place to place on beaches. During the winter, strong waves may wash away most of a beach's sand, leaving only gravel. The following summer, the waves slowly replace the sand.

During storms, waves can bring hundreds of tons of water crashing onto the shoreline, greatly eroding it. In France, storm waves once moved a 59,000-kg (65-ton) concrete block 20 m (65 ft). Powerful waves have been known to toss rocks weighing 45 kg (100 lbs).

Waves can be fun for surfing, for swimming, or just for watching. But because of all the energy they carry, they can also be very destructive. Later in this unit you'll find out how we have learned to harness the energy in waves. ■

INVESTIGATE FURTHER!

RESEARCH

Recall that tsunamis are huge ocean waves that can be extremely destructive as they approach land. Find out where these waves are most likely to occur and how people are warned about them. Report what you find out to the class.

INVESTIGATION 2

1. How are waves formed?

2. Would you expect larger waves to form from a wind with a fetch of 1 km or 3 km? Explain your answer.

WHAT CAUSES TIDES?

What never stops moving, is always going through a phase, is billions of years old, and yet becomes new again each month? If you know the answer to this riddle, then you know what causes the tides to rise and fall each day!

Activity
Making a Tide Model

What does the Moon's position have to do with the tides?

MATERIALS
- 2 cardboard circles
- tape
- marker or pen
- string
- cardboard sheet
- *Science Notebook*

Procedure

1. **Label** one side of the larger circle with the numbers 1–4, as shown in the picture.

2. Use the larger circle to model Earth and the smaller circle to model the Moon. Place a sheet of cardboard on a level surface. Then place Earth in the center of the cardboard, with number 1 facing right. Tie the ends of a piece of string together and position it so the string evenly circles Earth. The string represents the ocean water on Earth.

3. Place the Moon outside the string 2–3 cm to the right of number 1. The Moon's gravity pulls on Earth's oceans, causing them to bulge outward on the side where the Moon is located and on

Step 1

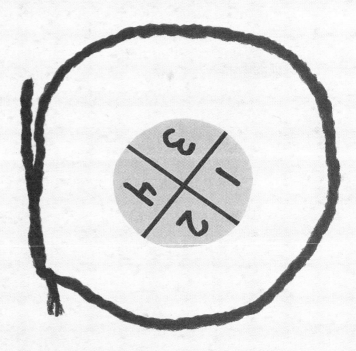

E68

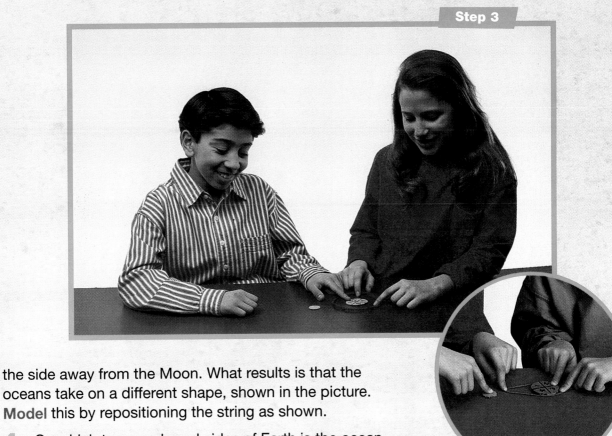

the side away from the Moon. What results is that the oceans take on a different shape, shown in the picture. **Model** this by repositioning the string as shown.

4. On which two numbered sides of Earth is the ocean deepest (in other words, bulging out farthest)? **Record** your answer. These sides are experiencing high tide. The two sides where the ocean is shallowest are experiencing low tide.

5. Trace a circle around Earth. Rotate Earth counter-clockwise until 1 moves to the position 3 used to be in. Be careful to keep Earth within the tracing without disturbing the string. You have just **modeled** the passing of about 6 hours in Earth's rotation. Leave Earth in this position.

Analyze and Conclude

1. In step 3, what was the relationship between the Moon's position and the high tides?

2. **Describe** how the tide changed at position 1 on Earth in step 5.

3. **Predict** how many high tides position 1, starting from its current location, will experience after one complete rotation of Earth occurs. **Test** your prediction.

4. **Suggest a hypothesis** to explain how the Moon causes tides.

INVESTIGATE FURTHER!

EXPERIMENT

Now consider the Sun's position. Cut a circle about twice the size of Earth's circle. Make sure it lines up with Earth and the Moon. Infer what the effect will be on Earth's oceans when the Sun is in this position. (Hint: Think about how the Moon causes tides.)

E69

The Moon, Sun, and Tides

The level of the oceans in a given place changes every day. These daily rises and falls in the ocean level are called **tides**. But did you know that tides are connected to the same force that causes falling leaves to drop to the ground?

Tides and the Moon's Gravity

It is the force of gravity that causes tides. In the tide model you constructed on pages E68 and E69, you probably inferred that the Moon's gravity pulls on Earth's oceans. The Moon's gravity pulls on the solid parts of Earth, too, but the effects of the pull are seen only in the rise and fall of water levels. Tides occur not only in oceans but in large rivers and bays as well.

The Moon's gravity pulls most strongly on the water facing the Moon, since this water is closest to the Moon. As a result, a bulge in the ocean called high tide

occurs. At the same time, the Moon's gravity pulls Earth itself away from the water on the opposite side of Earth. So a second bulge, or another high tide, occurs at the same time on the opposite side of Earth.

Because Earth rotates on its axis every 24 hours, most shores have two high tides a day. One high tide occurs when the Moon is on the same side of Earth as that shore. The second high tide occurs when the Moon is on the other side of Earth. Notice on the diagram that water is pulled away from the areas between the two high tides. As a result, most shores also have two low tides a day.

Actually, as Earth rotates, the Moon is moving in its orbit. It takes 24 hours and 50 minutes for a particular place in the ocean to pass under the Moon twice. This means that the tide pattern repeats itself every 24 hours and 50 minutes rather than every 24 hours.

The Sun's Role

The Sun's gravity also pulls on Earth. Although the Sun is much bigger than the Moon, it is also much farther away from Earth. Because of this greater distance,

◀ **The side of Earth facing the Moon experiences high tide. At the same time, a second high tide occurs on the other side of Earth.**

▲ Spring tide

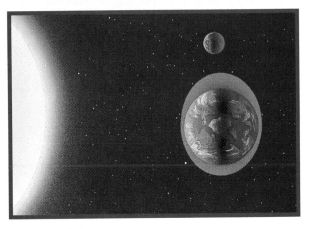

▲ Neap tide

the effect of the Sun's pull is less than that of the Moon's pull in producing tides.

You know that the Moon moves around Earth and Earth moves around the Sun. As a result, their positions are always changing. The Moon, Earth, and Sun line up twice a month—when the Moon is full and when it is new. During this time, the Moon and Sun pull together on Earth's oceans, much like two people pulling on a tug-of-war rope. The result is high tides that are *very* high and low tides that are *very* low. These extreme tides are called **spring tides**. (Here, *spring* refers to the "springing up" of the water, not the spring season.)

When the Sun and Moon are at a 90° angle with Earth, they no longer pull in the same direction. The pull of the Sun works against the pull of the Moon. As a result, high tides are not so high and low tides are not so low. These less extreme tides are called **neap tides**. Like spring tides, neap tides occur twice each month, when the Moon is in its first quarter and its third quarter phases. (In the activity you did on pages E68 and E69, how could you have modeled a neap tide?)

People and Tides

Tide charts have been developed to show the times for high and low tides each day at specific shores. Boaters and shell seekers check these charts to find out the best times to launch their boats or visit the beach. Special warnings are

The success of the D-Day invasion was dependent upon landing Allied troops during the lowest possible tide. On June 5 and 6, 1944, those conditions existed. The invasion took place on June 6, 1944.

E71

issued for storms that occur during high tides.

During World War II, the timing of the tides determined the date and time of the D-Day invasion. On June 6, 1944, the Allied forces landed on the beaches at Normandy, France. The invasion was planned for the lowest tide possible. That way, much of the beach would be exposed to make the landing safer.

The difference between the water levels at high tide and low tide is called the tidal range. In the open ocean, the tidal range is about 0.55 m (1.8 ft). When the incoming tide has room to spread out, as in the Gulf of Mexico, the tidal range may be only a few centimeters. Sometimes the incoming tide is forced into a small bay with steep sides. In this case, the water level may rise as much as 18 m (60 ft) during high tide. In addition, the tidal range at one place can change from one season to the next.

Century after century, the tides follow their own schedules, determined by the relative positions of the Moon, the Sun, and Earth. They are one of nature's tremendous forces, powerful enough to move entire oceans of water. ■

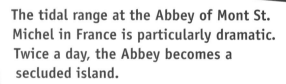

The tidal range at the Abbey of Mont St. Michel in France is particularly dramatic. Twice a day, the Abbey becomes a secluded island.

INVESTIGATION 3

THINK IT
WRITE IT

1. Use a sketch to show how the Moon's gravity causes tides on Earth.

2. How many low tides do most shore areas on Earth have during two days and two nights? Explain your answer.

REFLECT & EVALUATE

WORD POWER

crest
current
fetch
neap tide
period
spring tide
Coriolis effect
turbidity current

tides
trade winds
upwelling
wavelength
waves
westerlies

 On Your Own
Review the terms in the list. Then use as many terms as you can to write a brief summary of the chapter.

With a Partner
Use the terms in the list to make a word-search puzzle. See if your partner can find the hidden terms and tell you what each one means.

BUILD YOUR PORTFOLIO

Write a news report about the water movements and changes you might observe at a beach during a 24-hour period.

Analyze Information

Study the drawing. Then name the ocean feature shown and describe how it forms.

Assess Performance

Design a way of modeling a turbidity current. Outline the materials you would use and the procedure you would follow. After your teacher has approved your outline, create your model.

Problem Solving

1. How can surface currents both aid and hinder the movement of ships?

2. Describe how a toy boat floating on the ocean would move as a wave passed by.

3. Lakes have tides, but we often don't notice because their tidal range is so small. Would you expect a lake's tidal range to be more noticeable during a spring tide or a neap tide? Explain your answer.

CHAPTER 4

OCEAN RESOURCES

Many useful things come from the oceans—food, valuable minerals, sources of energy, and even fresh water. Yet much of this vast resource is being destroyed by pollution. What can you do to help save the oceans?

Learning About Our Friends

You may be aware of an ocean mammal that is popular with people—the incredible dolphin! People have come to have a special relationship with these playful mammals. Their intelligence and memory rank with the chimpanzees and the elephants.

In the photograph young Steven Clever listens in on "dolphin talk" at the Dolphin Quest Learning Center on the Big Island of Hawaii. The clicks he hears are sonar signals, which enable a dolphin to locate objects at night or in murky water.

Each year thousands of children visit this educational center. They learn that a great number of dolphins face the threat of death from toxic chemicals and garbage that is thrown into the water. This pollution occurs most often near the coastline homes of dolphins. Protecting the ocean helps protect the environment of these fascinating creatures.

▲ Steven Clever and his new friends at
the Dolphin Quest Learning Center

INVESTIGATION ①

WHAT RESOURCES CAN THE OCEANS PROVIDE?

There are many useful things that come from the sea. Did you know that ice cream and pudding contain a product that comes from plantlike organisms in the ocean? There are even farms floating on the sea that may provide some of your food. Find out about resources from the ocean in this investigation.

Activity

What You See From the Sea

Materials made from ocean resources are all around you. How many can you spot?

Procedure

Look around the classroom. Do you see anything you use that comes from the sea? Can you think of anything else you use that comes from the sea? Look around the rest of the building and your home. In your *Science Notebook* **make a list** of everything you find that comes from the sea. Be creative and make a poster to present your list.

Analyze and Conclude

1. How many items were you able to think of? How do the items on your list compare with items other students listed?

2. Make an **inference** regarding the importance of the sea to your life, based on all the observations your class made.

E76

Activity

Desalination

The ocean can be used as a fresh-water resource. How difficult is it to remove salt from ocean water?

Procedure

1. Pour a small amount of ocean water into a beaker. Cover the beaker with a plate.

2. Place the beaker under a lamp so that it is just below the lamp bulb. Turn on the lamp. Be careful not to touch the bulb or the lampshade.

Step 2

3. Leave the lamp on for 30 minutes.

4. Shut the lamp off and allow the setup to cool for 15 minutes. **Record** any changes you observe in the setup.

Analyze and Conclude

1. What collected on the plate? **Infer** how the matter differs from the ocean water and how it got on the plate.

2. How do you think your setup differs from a large-scale method to produce fresh water from ocean water? Could you use your method to efficiently produce fresh water from sea water? Why or why not?

Activity
Obtaining Energy

What kinds of energy might the oceans provide?

Procedure

1. Think of all the ways energy is produced. What raw materials are needed? What kinds of equipment are used to change the raw materials to usable forms of energy? In your *Science Notebook* **list** as many forms of energy as you can.

2. Think about oceans and their resources. **Hypothesize** about what untapped forms of energy there might be in the ocean. Be creative when listing ideas for obtaining energy from the oceans.

3. Choose one energy-source idea and **create a model** or a poster about it. Use any materials available. Be prepared to present your model or poster to the class. **Explain** what you are using from the ocean and how you plan to convert it to energy that people can use.

Step 3

Analyze and Conclude

1. **Describe** any problems you think your energy source may have that might keep it from being used. For example, is it practical for people living far inland as well as for people living near the ocean?

2. Which idea presented by your classmates do you think is the best idea? **Explain** your answer.

UNIT PROJECT LINK

The oceans provide a great variety of food products, including fish, shellfish, and seaweed. Research which life forms thrive near the site of your undersea lodge. Could some of these forms of life provide ocean farming products? Which ones? Why do you think so? Add pushpins and labels to your map to show possible areas for ocean farms. Also, diagram an idea you have for aquaculture technology. For example, you might show where and how young fish can be confined and fed until they mature.

Treasures From the Sea

With some practice, most people can learn to catch a fish. All you have to do is stand in the water, wait until a big one swims by, and scoop it up. That's how bears catch salmon in Alaska; it's also how early humans caught fish.

Food from the Sea

Today commercial fishing is much different from what it was in the past. If you were the captain of a modern fishing boat, you'd use sonar to find a school of fish, such as herring. The crew would spread huge nets in the water and then haul the whole school on board at once. No fuss, no muss—your ship could catch up to 36,400 kg (about 40 T) in one grab, enough to make fish dinners for 40,000 people! That school of herring has met its match!

What's the point? Well, seafood is probably the single most important resource we obtain from the ocean. In fact, more than half the protein eaten in Japan comes from the ocean.

Although some countries, such as the United States, may not depend on the ocean quite so heavily, the ocean is still an important source of food. What different kinds of seafood did you include on your list in the activity on page E76?

Modern fishing methods, like sonar, have almost made us *too* good at fishing. Many species of sea life have been overfished putting those species in danger of becoming extinct. Today, many fishing countries are reducing the amount of fish taken to protect this food resource before some species are gone.

▲ **Humans are not alone in harvesting the treasures of the sea. We share what is available with a wide variety of plants and animals.**

▲ Increasing demand for food worldwide has created a need for fish farming.

▲ As world population increases, the need for fresh water will probably force us to rely on desalination plants.

In addition to reducing the rate at which some species are being depleted, scientists hope to find alternative methods of obtaining ocean resources for food. A method called **aquaculture** (ak′wə kul chər), or ocean farming, will help the world meet growing food needs without overfishing. Aquaculture involves raising animals and seaweed in closed-off areas of the oceans and other waters. Organisms being farmed include lobsters, salmon, kelp, oysters, and mussels.

"Water, water everywhere, nor any drop to drink."

As Earth's population continues to increase, the rate at which fresh water is being used also is increasing. That's why, with so many oceans surrounding us, getting fresh water from salt water seems like a reasonable goal.

Obtaining fresh water from salt water is called **desalination** (dē sal ə nā′shən). However, only a few nations currently operate desalination plants. In the activity on page E77, the method that you used to remove salt from water was not very efficient. Large-scale operations are more efficient but they involve tremendous start-up and running costs. Often the cost of the energy needed to desalinate the ocean water would make the fresh water too expensive.

There is another possible source of fresh water in the oceans. Of all Earth's water, less than 3 percent is fresh, and 77 percent of this water is locked up in icecaps and glaciers. So it might make sense to attach cables to icebergs, tow them to where the water is needed, and pump the ice ashore as slush.

Common Chemicals from the Sea

In addition to water, what other chemicals do the oceans provide? About 30 percent of the world's salt supply comes directly from sea water. Giant factories along some coasts extract it by evaporating the ocean water.

More than 99 percent of the world's supply of bromine comes from the oceans. It's used in the manufacture of gasolines, dyes, medicines, and metals.

Even ocean food sources provide more than just food. For example, seaweed and kelp have been important foods in the Far East for hundreds of years. But seaweed provides other valuable products, too. Red seaweed yields agar, a product that dissolves in boiling water to make a clear gel. As a food additive, agar is used in canned meat, cake icing, candy, pet food, and any number of other foods. It's good for coating pills and for making cosmetics and is used in medical laboratories to grow bacteria, molds, and tissues. Brown seaweed produces alginic acid, which is used as a thickener in ice cream, jellies and pie fillings, salad dressings, shampoos, fabric dyes, plastics, rubber, and paints.

Animals from the sea make many non-food contributions. Blowfish toxin is a perfect example. If eaten, it can kill in 30 minutes. Yet when used medically, it is an extremely powerful painkiller. Another substance, produced by sea cucumbers, reduces tumors and may someday be used to fight cancer. The inedible parts of fish, including bones, are ground up for use in fertilizers and livestock feed.

Minerals and Fossil Fuels

Even the mud and ooze on the bottom of the oceans and seas are rich in resources. The floor of the Red Sea is covered with mud that contains tons of

▲ Alginic acid, which is obtained from brown kelp (*inset*), is used in the manufacture of products such as those shown here.

iron, zinc, copper, and silver, worth billions of dollars. Although these resources can't yet be mined because of the expense, scientists are researching ways to remove these materials cheaply.

When you ride in a car, you may be using another ocean resource. More than 20 percent of the world's oil and gas reserves are located under the ocean floor. From offshore oil rigs, workers drill down through sediment and rock to reach reserves of these fossil fuels. In addition to gasoline, chemicals taken from oil are used to make more than 3,000 products, including heating oil, plastics, detergents, and shampoos.

Think back to the list you created in the activity on page E76. How many of the treasures from the sea mentioned here did you include on your list? ■

◀ Agar, which is obtained from red kelp (*inset*), is used in the manufacture of products such as those shown here.

Treasures Through Time

You may enjoy eating fish or even wearing jewelry made from shells. But did you know that people have been mining the oceans for thousands of years? Ocean resources have been considered valuable treasures for a very long time! Explore some of them in this time line. ■

100 B.C.
Native American women in the Pacific Northwest gather foods from the sea floor.

1400 A.D.
Early forms of aquaculture are practiced along the coast of Indonesia.

By carrying large stones that make them sink to the sea floor, divers gather pearls in the Mediterranean Sea.
1000 B.C.

2700 B.C.
Poisonous fish are used as medicine in China.

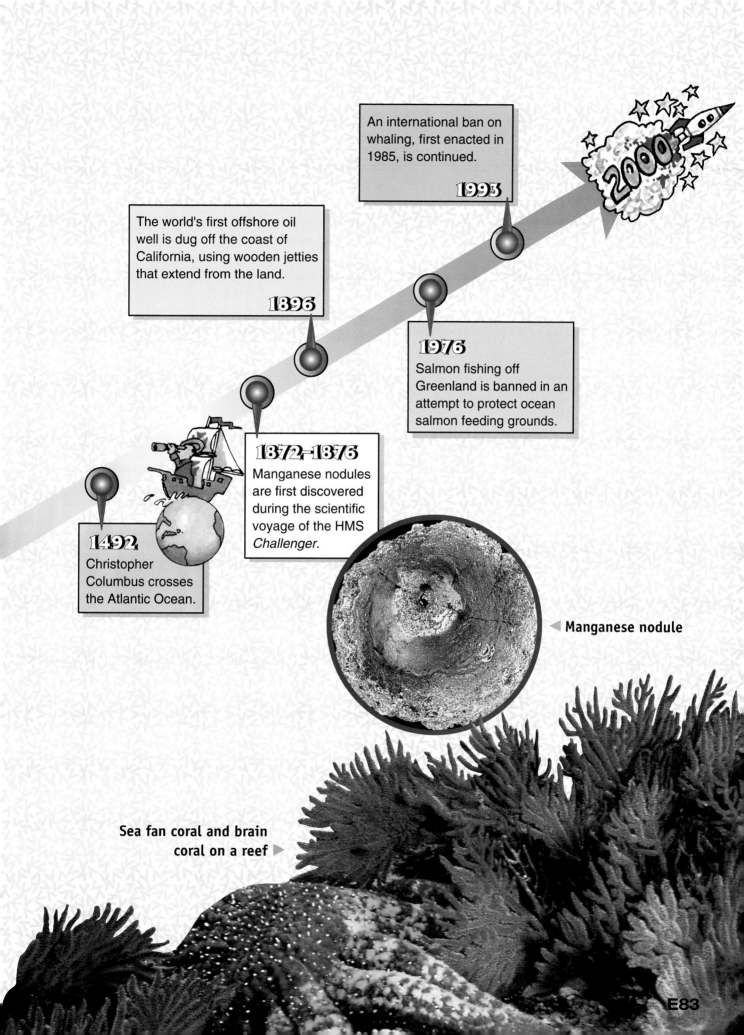

An international ban on whaling, first enacted in 1985, is continued.

1993

2000

The world's first offshore oil well is dug off the coast of California, using wooden jetties that extend from the land.

1896

1976

Salmon fishing off Greenland is banned in an attempt to protect ocean salmon feeding grounds.

1872–1876

Manganese nodules are first discovered during the scientific voyage of the HMS *Challenger.*

1492

Christopher Columbus crosses the Atlantic Ocean.

◄ **Manganese nodule**

Sea fan coral and brain coral on a reef ►

E83

Energy and the Sea

▲ **Just standing in a breaking wave can give you an idea of the tremendous energy that waves contain.**

For centuries people have stood on the ocean shore, marveled at the majesty of the waves, and dreamed of using that raw power. But other energy sources were cheaper and easier to use. Over the last few decades, however, the prices of coal, oil, and gas have soared, and some people have started looking to the sea for new sources of energy.

Power from the Waves

The Sun, winds, and oceans all produce enormous amounts of energy. So how do we harness all of this power? Recall that waves form when ocean water receives energy from the wind. If you have ever been swimming in the ocean, you know about the energy and power of waves. Water in a breaking wave can knock you over! So it makes sense to conclude that there is usable energy in waves.

Modern computers can calculate how much energy a moving section of ocean water should be able to provide.

1 **The ducks** ride the ocean surface, with the angled sides facing incoming waves. A rounded bottom dangles beneath the surface.

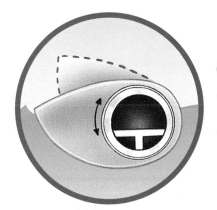

2 **Incoming waves** hit the hollow, concrete ducks; the angled sides tilt up, absorb the wave's energy, and then drop back down. So much of the wave's energy is absorbed that calm water is left behind the ducks. The energy of the bobbing movement turns a shaft running through a line of ducks.

SALTER'S DUCKS

The energy stored in 1 m (3 ft) of a typical wave in the Atlantic Ocean could provide about 70 kilowatts (kW) of power, enough to run 70 electric heaters. But several problems must be solved before that energy can be used.

First, obtaining energy from waves is 10 to 20 times more expensive than obtaining energy from other sources. Second, waves are rarely of a constant size for long periods of time, so their power is never constant. Additionally, even in calm areas of the ocean, storms can create waves capable of destroying even the strongest of energy collection devices in just a few minutes or hours. Third, no one has yet thought of a way to store wave energy for later use.

Nevertheless, many ideas for harnessing wave energy are being tested. A promising one involves Salter's ducks, devices named after their inventor, Stephen Salter. Study the diagrams to see how these devices work.

3 **Inside the shaft**, the absorbed energy moves oil through an engine, driving an electric generator. An 800-m (0.5-mi) string of ducks could supply energy for a city of 85,000 people.

OTEC

Other devices now being tested can take advantage of relatively small differences in ocean water temperatures. The method of using temperature differences to get energy from ocean water is called Ocean Thermal Energy Conversion, or OTEC.

In tropical areas the Sun may heat the ocean surface water to 27°C (81°F). But ocean water found at a depth of 610 m (2,000 ft) or more may be much colder. As shown in the drawing, the difference in temperature between the water at the ocean's surface and the deep water can be harnessed to power an engine that produces electricity.

Methane

As you have learned, the oceans are a major source of oil and natural gas. These fossil fuels are found in sediments and rocks below the ocean floor. But another kind of gas may be obtained from organisms living in ocean waters. This gas is called methane.

Methane is a colorless, odorless, burnable gas produced from the decomposition of organic matter. Rotting seaweed (such as kelp) and other kinds of algae are especially good sources of methane gas, since they are rich in hydrogen and carbon, the components of methane.

A Navy scientist, Howard Wilcox, has come up with a plan for growing kelp for use in making methane gas. He proposes that kelp be grown in open-ocean farms anchored on a series of plastic lines up to 31 m (102 ft) below the ocean surface. Wilcox believes that up to 50 percent of the energy in the kelp can be turned into methane fuel. An ocean farm of about 400 km² (154 mi²) could provide enough methane gas to power a city of 500,000 people.

Think back to the activity you did on page E78. Did you think of any methods

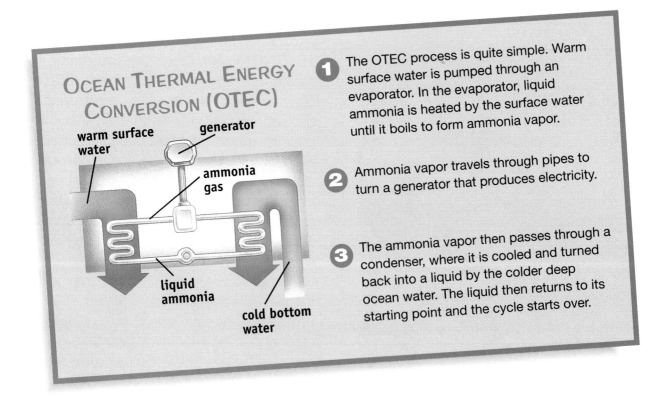

OCEAN THERMAL ENERGY CONVERSION (OTEC)

warm surface water

generator

ammonia gas

liquid ammonia

cold bottom water

1 The OTEC process is quite simple. Warm surface water is pumped through an evaporator. In the evaporator, liquid ammonia is heated by the surface water until it boils to form ammonia vapor.

2 Ammonia vapor travels through pipes to turn a generator that produces electricity.

3 The ammonia vapor then passes through a condenser, where it is cooled and turned back into a liquid by the colder deep ocean water. The liquid then returns to its starting point and the cycle starts over.

▲ As you can see in these pictures, the power of water cannot be overestimated. How can tidal energy be harnessed?

for obtaining energy from the ocean that are similar to the ones mentioned here?

Tidal Energy

An ancient myth tells of a king who thought he had grown so powerful he could command the seas. So he went to the ocean's edge, told the tide to stop moving . . . and drowned.

Unlike the king, modern scientists know they can't control the tides. But they have made astonishing progress toward finding ways to use tidal energy. If there is at least a 4.6-m (15-ft) difference between low and high tide, scientists think that the ebb and flow can be harnessed to produce usable energy.

The best-known tidal energy project is a power plant built at the mouth of the Rance (räns) River in France. Known as the Rance Tidal Power Station, the plant consists of 24 separate tunnels, each facing the sea and built into a dam stretching 702 m (2,303 ft) across the river. As the tide moves upriver, the tidal water flows through the tunnels and builds up behind the dam. At peak high tide the water is released and flows back to the sea, turning turbines connected to massive generators.

The Rance Power Station can generate up to 608 million kilowatt-hours (kWh) of electrical energy a year. However, the plant didn't pay its way at first and was almost shut down. Then in the 1970s, rising energy prices made its production costs seem more reasonable. ■

INVESTIGATION 1

1. Name six resources that come from the oceans.

2. Would tidal energy be a good source of energy for the town you live in? Why or why not?

INVESTIGATION 2

HOW DOES POLLUTION AFFECT THE OCEANS AND THEIR RESOURCES?

You now know that the oceans are a very large and very valuable resource. Now consider that pollution is damaging large parts of that resource. Explore the effects of ocean pollution in this investigation.

Activity
Investigating Oil Spills

What problems do oil spills create? To find out, observe how oil affects water and a feather.

- - - - - - - - - - - - - - - - - - -

Procedure

1. Work with a partner. Half-fill one container with water.

2. **Predict** what will happen if you place a small drop of oil in the water. **Record** your prediction in your *Science Notebook*.

3. **Test your prediction.** Using a spoon, place a small drop of oil in the water. How does the oil behave? **Record** what you observe.

Step 1

4. Place several more drops of oil in the water. Put the lid on the container, then carefully shake the container so that the water moves around. How do the oil and water interact? **Record** your observations. Save this container for the activity on page E90.

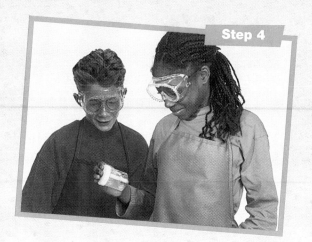
Step 4

5. Use a hand lens to examine a feather. **Record** your observations.

6. Fill another container with water. Soak the feather in the water for 1 minute. Remove it and blot it dry with a paper towel. Repeat step 5, using this feather.

7. Fill another container with oil to a depth of 1 cm. Soak the feather in the oil for 1 minute. Remove it and blot it dry with a paper towel. Repeat step 5, using this feather.

8. Dispose of the oil and water as directed by your teacher. Do not pour the oil and water down the drain.

Analyze and Conclude

1. From your observations, **infer** why it might be important to begin cleaning up an oil spill as soon as possible. What problems might a delay create?

2. What effect might an oil spill have on coastal birds?

3. Based upon your observations, **infer** why it is important to properly dispose of the oil used in this and the next activity. Why shouldn't you just pour it down the drain?

INVESTIGATE FURTHER!

EXPERIMENT

Predict the effect an oil spill might have on bird eggs in nests along the coast. Then test your prediction by soaking a hard-boiled egg in oil for 20 minutes. Remove the egg and blot it dry with a paper towel. Peel the egg and record your observations. Do not eat the egg.

Activity
Cleaning Up the Mess

You've seen some of the problems oil spills create. What is the best way to clean up an oil spill?

Procedure

1. Use the container of oil and water from step 4 of the previous activity as your model oil spill. Add a few more drops of oil to the water.

2. **Hypothesize** as to a method you might use to clean up the oil. **Record** your hypothesis in your *Science Notebook*.

3. **Experiment** to test your cleanup method. Begin by describing the procedure in detail. Then use any of the materials available to test your method.

4. As you test your method, place any oil or oily materials in the empty container. **Report** on how effective your method was.

5. Repeat steps 2 and 3 two more times, using either different materials or procedures. If needed, add more oil to the water.

Analyze and Conclude

1. **Describe** how difficult it was to clean up the oil spill.

2. Which method worked best? Why?

3. **Infer** how difficult it might be to use your method or one similar to it to clean up an oil spill in the ocean.

Step 3

Pollution of the Oceans

▲ This water may look pure, but the chances are very good that this water is polluted to some extent.

Pollution is the contamination of the environment with waste. When you realize that the water in practically every lake, river, and stream in the world eventually reaches the sea, it's not hard to figure out how our oceans become polluted.

For thousands of years, wastes, both liquid and solid, have been dumped into bodies of water. Even the waste thought to have been safely buried has found its way into underground streams and eventually to the oceans.

Since the nineteenth century, when people began mass-producing most goods, wastes from manufacturing have

Not all pollution is this obvious. Sometimes pollution is dissolved in the water and is impossible to see. ▼

E91

been dumped into the oceans in larger and larger amounts. As a result, the oceans and the life forms in them have been disturbed in very serious ways.

The Chain of Ocean Life

The oceans contain important ecosystems, in which all organisms and the wastes of some varieties of life are used by other organisms. At the beginning of the ocean food chain are microscopic organisms called phytoplankton. They float in the ocean and use sunlight to produce energy, absorbing carbon dioxide from the ocean water and the water itself in the process. Microscopic animal-like organisms, called zooplankton, eat the phytoplankton, and then are eaten in turn by small fish and some whales. The small fish are consumed by larger fish, which may then be consumed by even larger fish, seals, dolphins, some whales, birds, and humans.

Pollutants taken in by some ocean organisms can be passed to others through the ocean's food chains. Thus the harmful effects spread through ocean ecosystems.

Pollution Sources

There are many different sources and kinds of ocean pollution. Ordinary people

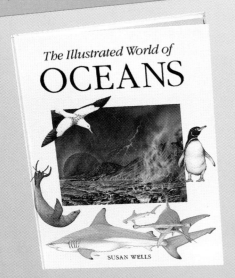

SCIENCE IN LITERATURE

The Illustrated World of
OCEANS

SUSAN WELLS

THE ILLUSTRATED WORLD OF OCEANS
by Susan Wells
Simon & Schuster Books for Young Readers, 1991

What ocean resource is most affected by our pollution? Most certainly, the living things. On pages 56–57 of *The Illustrated World of the Oceans*, you'll find out how chemicals from farming and industry affect ocean creatures. You'll also find out how plastics, which harm ocean animals, end up in the ocean.

Then, before you give up hope, read pages 58–59. Find out how people around the world are taking action to reduce ocean pollution and preserve ocean animals that are in danger. What actions can you take to help reduce ocean pollution?

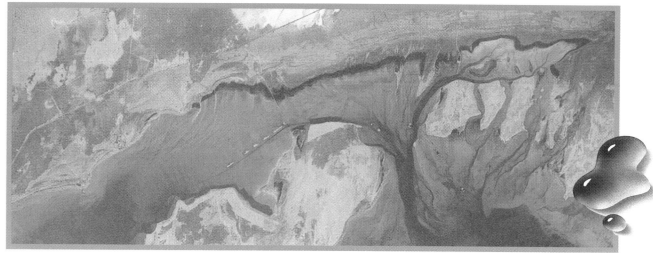

▲ This photo, taken in Spring 1991 by shuttle astronauts 256 km (138 mi) above the Strait of Hormuz, dramatically shows the extent of oil spilled during the Gulf War. The light sheen on the water is oil that has been dumped into the Strait.

are responsible for pollution, for all towns and cities produce sewage, both treated and raw. Few, if any, major industries in the world are entirely nonpolluting—almost all generate waste. Even farmers contribute dangerous chemicals in the form of pesticides and fertilizers that eventually make their way into the oceans by way of streams and rivers.

Toxic pollutants are poisonous chemicals that can cause sickness or death. In the 1950s mercury was dumped from a factory into the ocean near the fishing village of Minamata, Japan. Contaminated fish that were caught and eaten by people of the village caused brain damage, physical deformities, and birth defects.

The effects of ocean pollution were never more terrible than in Minamata, Japan, where mercury pollution caused brain damage and physical deformities. ▼

Ocean Oil Spills

Seemingly worst of all—but only because they are so much more visible than most forms of pollution—are the gigantic ocean spills of oil. When you modeled an oil spill on page E88, you inferred how oil spills can affect oceans.

Between 1967 and 1989, the 15 largest oil spills in the world spewed more than 14 million barrels of oil into the oceans. Most of the oil came from huge tankers rupturing on rocks or reefs. The best known occurred in 1989, when the *Exxon Valdez*, in a navigational error, ripped itself open on a reef in a huge, unspoiled bay in Alaska. Thousands of birds, fish, sea otters, whales, and dolphins died almost immediately by swallowing the oil. Others died slow deaths caused by respiratory distress or contamination of their fur or feathers.

Reducing Pollution!

Thankfully, many of the antipollution laws passed since the 1960s have had good results. Many industries have become extremely careful about adding more pollution to the oceans after realizing how serious the problem was. Now many areas along ocean shores, once badly polluted, are free of waste contamination. The pollution problem is not hopeless, though at times the outlook may seem bad.

As many people have noted, the only good way to deal with ocean pollution is to make sure it never happens. ■

Much of the pollution resulting from the *Exxon Valdez* accident has been cleaned up through the efforts of volunteers.

INVESTIGATION 2

1. Name three kinds of pollution that affect the oceans.

2. Describe why you do or do not think ocean pollution threatens the quality of all life on Earth.

REFLECT & EVALUATE

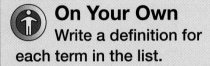

WORD POWER

aquaculture
desalination
pollution

On Your Own
Write a definition for each term in the list.

With a Partner
Mix up the letters of each term in the list. Provide a clue for each term and challenge your partner to unscramble the terms.

BUILD YOUR PORTFOLIO

Draw diagrams or create models showing ocean resources being obtained and later used. You might also create a display of different ways in which ocean resources are used.

Analyze Information

The photograph below shows one event involving pollution that might affect ocean life. Predict how this event might affect the entire food chain.

Assess Performance

Use the materials from the activities on pages E88 through E90 to design a method for limiting the spread of an oil spill during a cleanup operation. Be sure to take into account all the ways that the oily water might move throughout the ocean.

Problem Solving

1. If you were trapped on a deserted island, how might you use a variety of ocean resources in order to survive?

2. How might toxic ocean pollution and overfishing have a similar effect on ocean life?

3. Compare and contrast the way we use ocean resources today with the way people in the past used ocean resources.

Throughout this unit you've investigated questions related to oceanography in these four chapters. How will you use what you've learned, and how will you share that information with others? Here are some ideas.

Hold a Big Event to Share Your Unit Project

Get ready to promote your vision of the undersea nature lodge. Cut a large opening in a big piece of cardboard. This will be the "picture window" that enables travelers in the deep-diving vehicle to observe the ocean environments. Use your knowledge of the oceans to create a "moving picture" of various kinds of ocean life, the effects of waves and currents, and the features of the ocean bottom as seen from inside the vehicle as it descends deeper into the ocean. Draw or paint the storyboards and tape them together in order. Next, prepare a taped narration to accompany the moving pictures. Set up on easels other posters and maps you have made. Now you're ready to go! As your classmates and guests watch, unroll the pictures and turn on the tape.

Research

In the past, many of the ocean food chains were harmed by the actions of humans. However, in recent years, people have been doing things to prevent further damage and to reverse the damage that has already been done. Read library books and magazine articles to find out what actions are being taken to protect the oceans and their food chains. Then present a report on the most appropriate and most effective.

Take Action

Substances on Earth's surface often end up being washed by rain into rivers, which then flow into the ocean. For one week, record everything on your small surface of Earth—your neighborhood—that may end up in the ocean. For example, you might include trash, oil spills, weed killer, or fertilizer. Combine your record with your classmates' records. Which substances from your community threaten the ocean? How? Create a poster ad to educate people about what they can do to protect the ocean.

SCIENCE

Handbook

THINK LIKE A SCIENTIST

You don't have to be a professional scientist to act and think like one. Thinking like a scientist mostly means using common sense. It also means learning how to test your ideas in a careful way.

In other words, you can think like a scientist.

Make a Hypothesis

Plan and Do a Test

Make Observations

To think like a scientist, you should learn as much as you can by observing things around you. Everything you hear and see is a clue about how the natural world works.

Ask a Question

Look for patterns. You'll get ideas and ask questions like these:

- Do all birds eat the same seeds?
- How does the time that the Sun sets change from day to day?

Make a Guess Called a Hypothesis

If you have an idea about why or how something happens, make an educated guess, or *hypothesis*, that you can test. For example, let's suppose that your hypothesis about the sunset time is that it changes by one minute each day.

Plan and Do a Test

Plan how to test your hypothesis. Your plan would need to consider some of these problems:

- How will you measure the time that the Sun sets?
- Will you measure the time every day?
- For how many days or weeks do you need to measure?

Record and Analyze What Happens

When you test your idea, you need to observe carefully and write down, or record, everything that happens. When you finish collecting data, you may need to do some calculations with it. For example, you might want to calculate how much the sunset time changes in a week or a month.

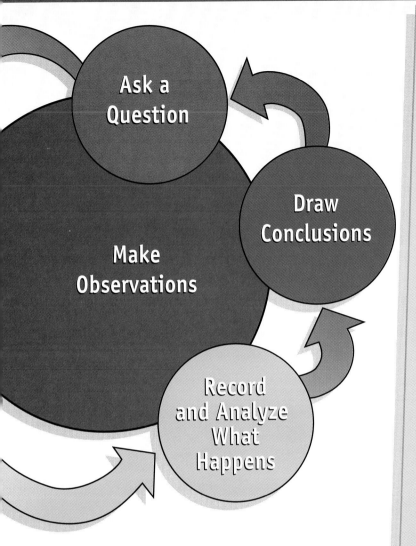

Ask a Question

Draw Conclusions

Make Observations

Record and Analyze What Happens

To think like a scientist, you need to practice certain ways of thinking.

Always check for yourself.
Always ask, "How do I really know it's true?" Be willing to find out for yourself.

Be honest and careful about what you observe.
It's easy to only look for the results you expect. It's harder to see the unexpected. But unexpected results lead scientists to ask more questions. They also provide information on how things work.

Don't be afraid to be wrong.
Based on their observations, scientists make many hypotheses. Not all of these hypotheses turn out to be correct. But scientists can learn from wrong "guesses," because even wrong guesses result in information that leads to knowledge.

Keep an open mind about possible explanations.
Make sure to think about all the reasons why something might have happened. Consider all the explanations that you can think of.

Draw Conclusions

Whatever happens in a test, think about all the reasons for your results. For example, you might wonder what causes the time of sunset to change. You might also ask when the earliest and latest sunsets occur during the year. Sometimes this thinking leads to a new hypothesis.

If the time of the sunset changes by one minute each day, think about what else the data shows you. Can you predict the time that the Sun will set one month from now?

DOES THE TEMPERATURE OF A LIQUID AFFECT HOW MUCH SOLUTE IT CAN HOLD?

Here's an example of an everyday problem and how thinking like a scientist can help you explore it.

"I can't believe it."

"It's true."

"It's impossible! Ten?"

"That's right."

"A cup of herbal tea can't hold ten teaspoons of sugar."

"My mother's does," replied Mark. "She likes it sweet."

"I'll bet most of the sugar just sinks to the bottom of the cup," Nita asserted. "Doesn't it?"

"No, it doesn't," Mark said. "Would I lie to you?"

"Listen," Nita said, "Ms. Cobb's been teaching us about solutions. I'll bet if I asked her she'd say it's impossible."

Make Observations

Ask a Question

Nita explained the issue to Ms. Cobb and the other students. She asked Ms. Cobb to give her opinion, but she wouldn't. She simply asked the class what they thought. Some students thought it was possible, others thought it was impossible. Ms. Cobb suggested that the class figure out a way to find the answer.

Ms. Cobb invited the students to come up with questions that expressed the problem they want to solve. Two of the questions were:

How much sugar can a cup of herbal tea hold?

Can hot water dissolve more sugar than cold water can?

Nita and Mark thought the second question was more interesting because it applied to more things—like coffee and lemonade. They were not sure what the answer to this question would be. But it was the kind of question that would tell them more about the nature of solutions.

Scientific investigations usually begin with something that you have noticed or read about. As you think about what you already know, you'll discover some ideas that you're not sure about. This will help you to ask the question that you really want to answer.

Make a Hypothesis

Mark and Nita talked the problem over. Mark told Nita that his mother drank her herbal tea very hot; she always waited until the water was boiling violently before pouring it into her cup. "Maybe," Nita said, "if the water wasn't so hot, it would hold less sugar." Mark agreed that this was possible. But he wasn't sure.

Mark and Nita had a hunch that the hotter water is, the more solute, such as sugar, the water will hold. They came up with a hypothesis, a statement of what they thought was true. Their hypothesis was "The hotter the water, the more sugar it will dissolve."

Nita and Mark got a few heat-proof glass beakers, a cup measure, and thermometers. Ms. Cobb got 1-teaspoon measuring spoons and a bowl of sugar from the school cafeteria. She also borrowed several hotplates. Ms. Cobb reviewed the test procedure that Mark and Nita had planned.

When you use what you have observed to suggest a possible answer to your question, you are making a *hypothesis*. Be sure that your hypothesis is an idea that you can test somehow. If you can't think of an experiment or a model to test your hypothesis, try changing it. Sometimes it's better to make a simpler, clearer hypothesis that answers only part of your question.

Plan and Do a Test

Make Observations

Mark and Nita knew they'd have to keep track of the different water temperatures in each beaker. They knew they'd have to put the same amount of water in each beaker. They would also have to keep track of how many teaspoons of sugar went into each beaker.

Nita knew that water boiled at 100 degrees Celsius (°C). So the beaker with the hottest water should be at this temperature. Another beaker could have water at 70°C; a third might have water at 40°C.

Mark suggested that they have a fourth beaker containing a cup of cold water at about 5°C—water whose temperature was close to freezing. This beaker would serve as their control. The control in this experiment would allow Mark and Nita to test the effect of heat on water's ability to dissolve sugar.

Ms. Cobb set up four water baths at the temperatures they agreed upon. Each was kept at a constant temperature. Each water bath had a thermometer in it.

One way to try out your hypothesis is to use a test called an experiment. When you plan an experiment, be sure that it helps you to answer your question. Even when you plan, things can happen that make the experiment confusing or make it not work properly. If this happens, you can change the plan for the experiment, and try again.

Record and Analyze What Happened

Make Observations

Mark and Nita asked two classmates to help them put teaspoons of sugar into the beakers. After each teaspoon of sugar went in, the solution was stirred with a glass stirring rod until the sugar dissolved. Each

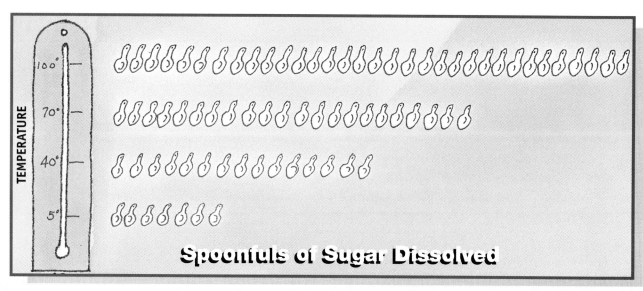

Spoonfuls of Sugar Dissolved

student kept track of the number of teaspoons of sugar that dissolved in it.

At the end of the experiment, each student looked at what he or she had written down. This information was organized in a graph like the one on page H6.

Mark and Nita studied the graph of the data they got during their experiment. They noticed that there was a definite relationship between water temperature and how much sugar could be dissolved in it.

Nita was surprised to see that Mark's mother's tea could really hold a lot more than 10 teaspoons of sugar. She and Mark agreed that people could drink their tea really sweet, unless, that is, they made it with cooler water.

Draw Conclusions

Make Observations

Mark and Nita decided that their test results supported their hypothesis. But they had noticed something odd that had happened in the beaker containing the hottest water. At some point after the water had cooled, a small amount of sugar added to the solution caused many sugar crystals to form.

They told Ms. Cobb about this strange result. Ms. Cobb congratulated them for having created a "supersaturated" solution. She suggested that Mark and Nita might want to plan another experiment to find out more about such solutions.

When you do an experiment, you need to write down, or record, your observations. Some of your observations might be numbers – things that you counted or measured. Your recorded observations are called data. When you record your data, you need to organize it in a way that helps you to understand it. Graphs and tables are helpful ways to organize data. Then think about the information you have collected. Analyze what it tells you.

After you have analyzed your data, you should use what you have learned to draw a conclusion. A conclusion is a statement that sums up what you learned. The conclusion should be about the question you asked. Think about whether the information you have gathered supports your hypothesis or not. If it does, figure out how to check out your idea more thoroughly. Also think about new questions you can ask.

SAFETY

The best way to be safe in the classroom is to use common sense. Prepare yourself for each activity before you start it. Get help from your teacher when there is a problem. Most important of all, pay attention. Here are some other ways that you can stay safe.

Stay Safe From Stains

- Wear protective clothing or an old shirt when you work with messy materials.
- If anything spills, wipe it up or ask your teacher to help you clean it up.

Stay Safe From Flames

- Keep your clothes away from open flames. If you have long or baggy sleeves, roll them up.
- Don't let your hair get close to a flame. If you have long hair, tie it back.

Stay Safe During Cleanup

- Wash up after you finish working.
- Dispose of things in the way that your teacher tells you to.

Stay Safe From Injuries

- Protect your eyes by wearing safety goggles when you are told that you need them.
- Keep your hands dry around electricity. Water is a good conductor of electricity, so you can get a shock more easily if your hands are wet.
- Be careful with sharp objects. If you have to press on them, keep the sharp side away from you.
- Cover any cuts you have that are exposed. If you spill something on a cut, be sure to wash it off immediately.
- Don't eat or drink anything unless your teacher tells you that it's okay.

MOST IMPORTANTLY

If you ever hurt yourself or one of your group members gets hurt, tell your teacher right away.

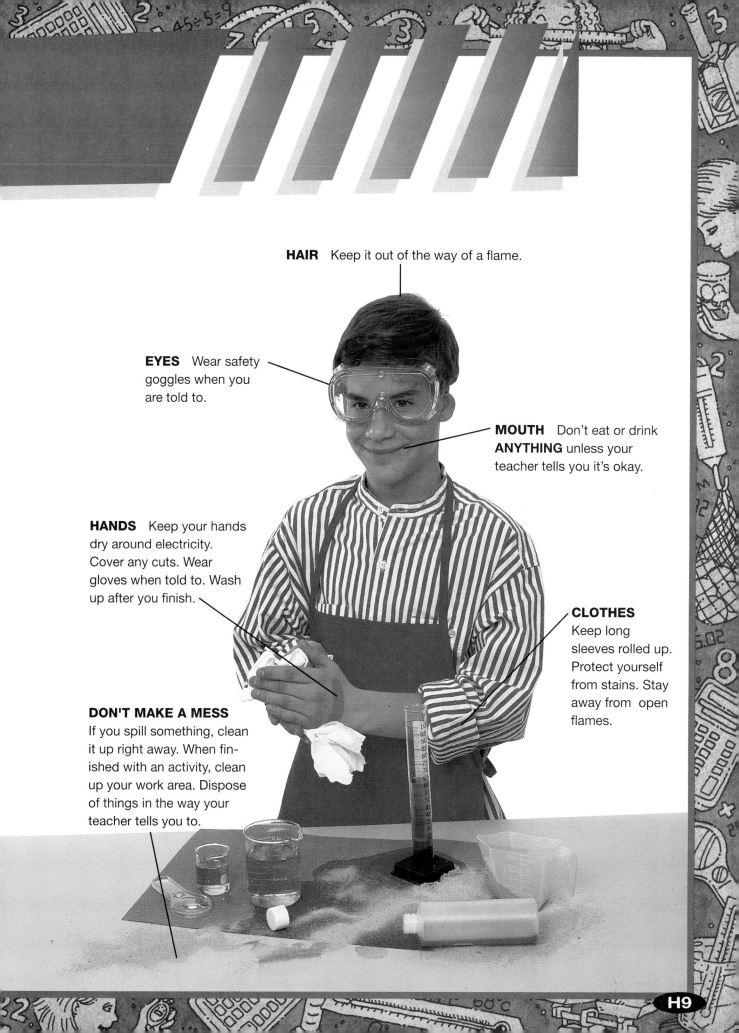

HAIR Keep it out of the way of a flame.

EYES Wear safety goggles when you are told to.

MOUTH Don't eat or drink **ANYTHING** unless your teacher tells you it's okay.

HANDS Keep your hands dry around electricity. Cover any cuts. Wear gloves when told to. Wash up after you finish.

CLOTHES Keep long sleeves rolled up. Protect yourself from stains. Stay away from open flames.

DON'T MAKE A MESS If you spill something, clean it up right away. When finished with an activity, clean up your work area. Dispose of things in the way your teacher tells you to.

Using a Microscope

A microscope makes it possible to see very small things by magnifying them. Some microscopes have a set of lenses to magnify objects different amounts.

Examine Some Salt Grains

Handle a microscope carefully; it can break easily. Carry it firmly with both hands and avoid touching the lenses.

1. Turn the mirror toward a source of light. **NEVER** use the Sun as a light source.

2. Place a few grains of salt on the slide. Put the slide on the stage of the microscope.

3. While looking through the eyepiece, turn the adjustment knob on the back of the microscope to bring the salt grains into focus.

4. Raise the eyepiece tube to increase the magnification; lower it to decrease magnification.

Using a
Calculator

After you've made measurements, a calculator can help you analyze your data. Some calculators have a memory key that allows you to save the result of one calculation while you do another.

Find an Average

The table shows the amount of rain that was collected using a rain gauge in each month of one year. You can use a calculator to help you find the average monthly rainfall.

1. Add the numbers. When you add a series of numbers, you don't need to press the equal sign until the last number is entered. Just press the plus sign after you enter each number (except the last one).

2. If you make a mistake while you are entering numbers, try to erase your mistake by pushing the clear entry (CE) key or the clear (C) key. Then you can continue entering the rest of the numbers you are adding. If you can't fix your mistake, you can push the (C) key once or twice until the screen shows 0. Then start over.

3. Your total should be 1,131. You can use the total to find the average. Just divide by the number of months in the year.

These keys run the calculator's memory functions.

This key erases the last entry.

Rainfall	
Month	Rain (mm)
Jan.	214
Feb.	138
Mar.	98
Apr.	157
May	84
June	41
July	5
Aug.	23
Sept.	48
Oct.	75
Nov.	140
Dec.	108

Using a Balance

A balance is used to measure mass. Mass is the amount of matter in an object. Place the object to be massed in the left pan. Place standard masses in the right pan.

Measure the Mass of an Orange

1. Check that the empty pans are balanced, or level with each other. The pointer at the base should be on the middle mark. If it needs to be adjusted, move the slider on the back of the balance a little to the left or right.

2. Place an orange on the left pan. Notice that the pointer moves and that the pans are no longer level with each other. Then add standard masses, one at a time, to the right pan. When the pointer is at the middle mark again, the pans are balanced. Each pan holds the same amount of mass.

3. Each standard mass is marked to show the number of grams it contains. Add the number of grams marked on the masses in the pan. The total is the mass in grams of the orange.

Using a Spring Scale

A spring scale is used to measure force. You can use a spring scale to find the weight of an object in newtons. You can also use the scale to measure other forces.

Measure the Weight of an Object

1. Place the object in a net bag, and hang it from the hook on the bottom of the spring scale. Or, if possible, hang the object directly from the hook.

2. Slowly lift the scale by the top hook. Be sure the object to be weighed continues to hang from the bottom hook.

3. Wait until the pointer on the face of the spring scale has stopped moving. Read the number next to the pointer to determine the weight of the object in newtons.

Measure Friction

1. Hook the object to the bottom of the spring scale. Use a rubber band to connect the spring scale and object if needed.

2. Gently pull the top hook of the scale parallel to the floor. When the object starts to move, read the number of newtons next to the pointer on the scale. This number is the force of friction between the floor and the object as you drag the object.

Using a
Thermometer

A thermometer is used to measure temperature. When the liquid in the tube of a thermometer gets warmer, it expands and moves farther up the tube. Different units can be used to measure temperature, but scientists usually use the Celsius scale.

Measure the Temperature of a Cold Liquid

1. Half-fill a cup with chilled liquid.

2. Hold the thermometer so that the bulb is in the center of the liquid.

3. Wait until you see the liquid in the tube stop moving. Read the scale line that is closest to the top of the liquid in the tube.

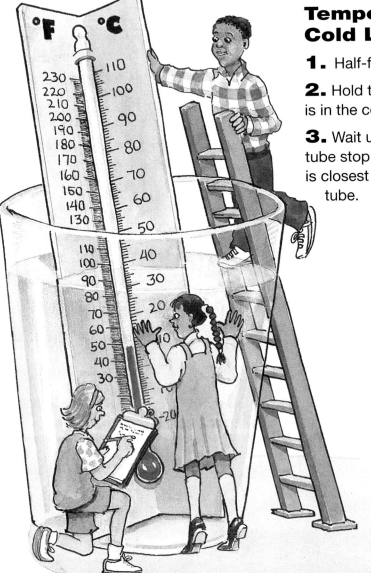

Measuring Volume

A graduated cylinder, a measuring cup, and a beaker are used to measure volume. Volume is the amount of space something takes up. Most of the containers that scientists use to measure volume have a scale marked in milliliters (mL).

Measure the Volume of Juice

1. Pour the juice into a measuring container.

2. Move your head so that your eyes are level with the top of the juice. Read the scale line that is closest to the surface of the juice. If the surface of the juice is curved up on the sides, look at the lowest point of the curve.

3. You can estimate the value between two lines on the scale to obtain a more accurate measurement.

▲ The bottom of the curve is at 50 mL.

This beaker has marks for each 25 mL. ▼

This graduated cylinder has marks for every 1 mL. ▶

This measuring cup has marks for each 25 mL. ▼

Each container above has 50 mL of juice.

MEASUR

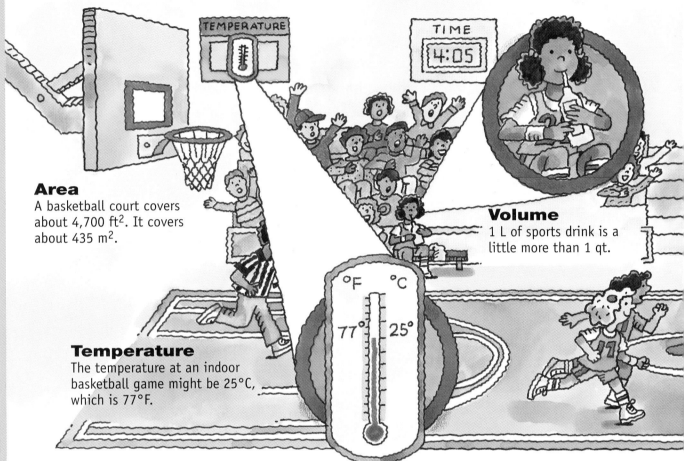

Area
A basketball court covers about 4,700 ft^2. It covers about 435 m^2.

Volume
1 L of sports drink is a little more than 1 qt.

Temperature
The temperature at an indoor basketball game might be 25°C, which is 77°F.

SI Measures

Temperature
Ice melts at 0 degrees Celsius (°C)

Water freezes at 0°C

Water boils at 100°C

Length and Distance
1,000 meters (m) = 1 kilometer (km)

100 centimeters (cm) = 1 m

10 millimeters (mm) = 1 cm

Force
1 newton (N) =
1 kilogram x meter/second/second
(kg x m/s^2)

Volume
1 cubic meter (m^3) = 1 m x 1 m x 1 m

1 cubic centimeter (cm^3) =
1 cm x 1 cm x 1 cm

1 liter (L) = 1,000 milliliters (mL)

1 cm^3 = 1 mL

Area
1 square kilometer (km^2) = 1 km x 1 km

1 hectare = 10,000 m^2

Mass
1,000 grams (g) = 1 kilogram (kg)

1,000 milligrams (mg) = 1 g

EMENTS

Mass and Weight
A basketball has a mass of about 650 g.
It weighs about $1\frac{1}{2}$ lb.

Length/ Distance
A basketball rim is about
10 ft high, or a little more
than 3 m from the floor.

Rates (SI and English)

km/h = kilometers per hour

m/s = meters per second

mph = miles per hour

English Measures

Volume of Fluids
8 fluid ounces (fl oz) = 1 cup (c)

2 c = 1 pint (pt)

2 pt = 1 quart (qt)

4 qt = 1 gallon (gal)

Temperature
Ice melts at 32 degrees
Fahrenheit (°F)

Water freezes at 32°F

Water boils at 212°F

Length and Distance
12 inches (in.) = 1 foot (ft)

3 ft = 1 yard (yd)

5,280 ft = 1 mile (mi)

Weight
16 ounces (oz) = 1 pound (lb)   2,000 pounds = 1 ton (T)

GLOSSARY

Pronunciation Key

Symbol	Key Words		Symbol	Key Words
a	cat		g	get
ā	ape		h	help
ä	cot, car		j	jump
			k	kiss, call
e	ten, berry		l	leg
ē	me		m	meat
			n	nose
i	fit, here		p	put
ī	ice, fire		r	red
			s	see
ō	go		t	top
ô	fall, for		v	vat
oi	oil		w	wish
oo	look, pull		y	yard
o͞o	tool, rule		z	zebra
ou	out, crowd			
			ch	chin, arch
u	up		ŋ	ring, drink
ʉ	fur, shirt		sh	she, push
			th	thin, truth
ə	a in ago		*th*	then, father
	e in agent		zh	measure
	i in pencil			
	o in atom			
	u in circus			
b	bed			
d	dog			
f	fall			

A heavy stress mark ′ is placed after a syllable that gets a heavy, or primary, stress, as in **picture** (pik′chər).

A

abyssal plain (ə bis′əl plān) The broad, flat ocean bottom. (E34) The *abyssal plain* covers nearly half of Earth's surface.

acceleration (ak sel er ā′shən) The rate at which velocity changes over time. (F21) The spacecraft's *acceleration* increased as it soared into the air.

acid (as′id) A compound that turns blue litmus paper to red and forms a salt when it reacts with a base. (C81) *Acids* have a sour taste.

action force The initial force exerted in a force-pair. (F92) When you push against something, you are applying an *action force.*

aftershock A less powerful shock following the principal shock of an earthquake. (B58) Many *aftershocks* shook the ground in the days after the major earthquake.

algae (al′jē) Any of various plantlike protists. (A35) Diatoms and seaweed are kinds of *algae.*

allergy (al′ər jē) An oversensitivity to a specific substance that is harmless to most people, such as pollen, dust, animal hair, or a particular food. (G42) An *allergy* may cause such symptoms as sneezing, itching, or a rash.

alloy (al′oi) A solution of two or more metals. (C59) Bronze is an *alloy* of copper and tin.

antibiotic (an tī bī ät′ik) A substance, produced by microbes or fungi, that can destroy bacteria or stop their growth. Also, a synthetic substance with these properties. (A59) Doctors prescribe *antibiotics* to treat various bacteria-caused diseases.

antibody (an′ti bäd ē) A protein produced in the blood that destroys or weakens bacteria and other pathogens. (A59, G35) *Antibodies* are produced in response to infection.

aquaculture (ak′wə kul chər) The raising of water plants and animals for human use or consumption. (E80) Raising catfish on a catfish "farm" is a form of *aquaculture.*

asexual reproduction Reproduction involving a cell or cells from one parent and resulting in offspring exactly like the parent. (D10) The division of an amoeba into two cells is an example of *asexual reproduction.*

asthenosphere (as then′ə sfir) The layer of Earth below the lithosphere; the upper part of the mantle. (B39) The *asthenosphere* contains hot, partially melted rock with plasticlike properties.

astronomical unit A unit of measurement equal to the distance from Earth to the Sun. (F9) Pluto is 39.3 *astronomical units* (A.U.) from the Sun.

atom The smallest particle of an element that has the chemical properties of that element. (C35) An *atom* of sodium differs from an *atom* of chlorine.

atomic number (ə täm′ik num′bər) The number of protons in the nucleus of an atom of an element. (C73) The *atomic number* of oxygen is 8.

─── ───

bacteria (bak tir′ē ə) Monerans that feed on dead organic matter or on living things. (A51, G33) Diseases such as pneumonia and tuberculosis are caused by *bacteria.*

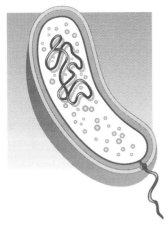

base A compound that turns red litmus paper blue and that forms a salt when it reacts with an acid. (C81) *Bases* have a slippery feel.

behavioral risk factor (bē hāv′yər əl risk fak′tər) A health risk factor that results from a person's choices about his or her lifestyle. (G53) Using drugs or alcohol is a *behavioral risk factor.*

benthos (ben′thäs) All the plants and animals that live on the ocean bottom. (E25) *Benthos* include oysters, crabs, and coral.

blue-green bacteria (bloō grēn bak tir′ē ə) Monerans that contain chlorophyll. (A51) Like plants, *blue-green bacteria* carry out photosynthesis and make their own food.

budding A form of asexual reproduction in which a new individual develops from a bump, or bud, on the body of the parent. (D13) Some one-celled organisms, such as yeast, reproduce by *budding.*

buoyancy (boi′ən sē) The tendency of fluids, like water, to keep objects afloat. (F123) Objects float better in salt water than in fresh water because salt water has greater *buoyancy.*

─── ───

caldera (kal der′ə) A large circular depression, or basin, at the top of a volcano. (B104) The eruption formed a *caldera* that later became a lake.

cast fossil (kast fäs′əl) A fossil formed when minerals from rock move into and harden within the space left by a decaying organism. (D57) *Cast fossils* of shells can provide information about the animals from which the fossils formed.

cell The basic unit that makes up all living things. (A9) The human body is made up of trillions of *cells.*

cell differentiation (sel dif ər en shē-ā'shən) The development of cells into different and specialized cell types. (A25) Through *cell differentiation*, plant and animal cells develop into tissues.

cell membrane (sel mem'brān) The structure that surrounds and encloses a cell and controls the movement of substances into and out of the cell. (A10) The *cell membrane* shrank when the cell was placed in salt water.

cell respiration (sel res pə rā'shən) The process in cells in which oxygen is used to release stored energy by breaking down sugar molecules. (A19) The process of *cell respiration* provides energy for a cell's activities.

cell theory A theory that states that cells are the basic units of structure and function of all living things. (A10) The *cell theory* states that new cells are produced from existing cells.

cell wall The rigid structure surrounding the cells of plants, monerans, and some protists. (A10) The *cell wall* gives a cell its rigid shape.

chemical bond A force, or link, that holds atoms together in a molecule or in a crystal. (C73) In a water molecule, atoms of hydrogen and oxygen are held together by *chemical bonds.*

chemical change A change in matter that results in new substances with new properties. (C69) A *chemical change* occurs when wood burns and forms gases and ash.

chemical formula A group of symbols and numbers that shows what elements make up a compound. (C40) The *chemical formula* for carbon dioxide is CO_2.

chemical properties Characteristics of matter that describe how it changes when it reacts with other matter. (C34) The ability to burn is a *chemical property* of paper.

chemical symbol One or two letters used to stand for the name of an element. (C36) Ca is the *chemical symbol* for calcium.

chloroplast (klôr'ə plast) A tiny green organelle that contains chlorophyll and is found in plant cells and some protist cells. (A10) The chlorophyll inside a *chloroplast* enables a plant cell to capture solar energy.

cholesterol (kə les'tər ôl) A fatty substance, found in foods, that can lead to clogged blood vessels. (G60) A diet that is too high in *cholesterol* can increase the risk of heart disease.

chromosome (krō'mə sōm) A threadlike structure in the nucleus of a cell; it carries the genes that determine the traits an offspring inherits from its parent or parents. (A10, D22, G12) Most cells in the human body contain 23 pairs of *chromosomes.*

cilia (sil'ē ə) Small, hairlike structures lining the membranes of the respiratory system. (G33) *Cilia* help to filter the air that enters the body.

cinder-cone volcano (sin′dər kōn väl kā′nō) A kind of volcano, usually small and steep-sloped, that is formed from layers of cinders, which are sticky bits of volcanic material. (B88) *Cinder-cone volcanoes* result from explosive eruptions.

communicable disease (kə myo͞o′ni-kə bəl di zēz) A disease that can be passed from one individual to another. (A58) Bacteria, which are easily passed from organism to organism, are the cause of many *communicable diseases.*

competition The struggle among organisms for available resources. (D77) *Competition* among members of a species is a factor in evolution.

composite-cone volcano (kəm pāz′it kōn väl cā′nō) A kind of volcano formed when explosive eruptions of sticky lava alternate with quieter eruptions of volcanic rock bits. (B89) Mount Vesuvius is a *composite-cone volcano* in southern Italy.

compound (käm′pound) A substance made up of two or more elements that are chemically combined. (C34) Water is a *compound* made up of hydrogen and oxygen.

condensation (kän dən sā′shən) The change of state from a gas to a liquid. (C28) The *condensation* of water vapor can form droplets of water on the outside of a cold glass.

continental edge (kän tə nent″l ej) The point at which the continental shelf, which surrounds each continent, begins to angle sharply downward. (E33) Beyond the *continental edge* the ocean increases rapidly in depth.

continental rise The lower portion of the continental slope, extending to the ocean floor. (E33) The *continental rise* usually starts angling down to the ocean floor about a mile beneath the ocean.

continental shelf The sloping shelf of land, consisting of the edges of the continents under the ocean. (E32) The *continental shelf* can extend hundreds of miles out into the ocean.

continental slope The steep clifflike drop from the continental edge to the ocean floor. (E33) The *continental slope* connects the continental shelf with the ocean bottom.

convection (kən vek′shən) The process by which heat energy is transferred through liquids or gases by the movement of particles. (B39) The pie in the oven was heated by *convection.*

convection current The path along which energy is transferred during convection. (B39) Scientists think that *convection currents* in the mantle cause Earth's tectonic plates to move.

convergent boundary (kən vur′jənt boun′də rē) A place where the plates that make up Earth's crust and upper mantle move together. (B40) Layers of rock may bend or break at a *convergent boundary.*

Coriolis effect (kôr ē ō′lis e fekt′) The tendency of a body or fluid moving across Earth's surface to have a curving motion due to Earth's rotation. (E56) The *Coriolis effect* causes air and water currents to move to the right in the Northern Hemisphere and to the left in the Southern Hemisphere.

crest The top of a wave. (E65) The *crest* of the wave seemed to tower over the surfer.

crust The thin outer layer of Earth. (B19) Earth's *crust* varies from 5 km to 48 km in thickness.

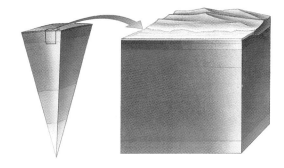

current Great rivers of water moving through the ocean. (E55) The *current* pulled the boat away from shore.

cytoplasm (sīt′ō plaz əm) The watery gel inside a cell. (A11) Various organelles are found inside the *cytoplasm* of a cell.

deceleration (dē sel ər ā′shən) A decrease in speed over time. (F23) Air resistance can cause the *deceleration* of objects.

density The amount of mass in a given volume of matter. (C13) Lead has a greater *density* than aluminum.

desalination (dē sal ə nā′shən) A process for obtaining fresh water from salt water by removing the salt. (E80) A few countries operate *desalination* plants, which obtain fresh water from ocean water.

diatom (dī′ə täm) A microscopic, one-celled alga with a glasslike cell wall. (A35) A single liter of sea water may contain millions of *diatoms.*

dietary fat A nutrient in food that provides energy. (G60) A small amount of *dietary fat* is part of a healthful diet.

diffusion (di fyōō′zhən) The tendency of substances to move from an area of greater concentration to an area of lesser concentration. (A16) Substances can pass in and out of cells by *diffusion.*

divergent boundary (di vur′jənt boun′də rē) A place where the plates that make up Earth's crust and upper mantle move away from one another. (B40) Most *divergent boundaries* are found on the floor of the ocean.

dome mountain A mountain formed when magma lifts Earth's surface, creating a broad dome, or bulge. (B47) Pikes Peak in Colorado is a *dome mountain.*

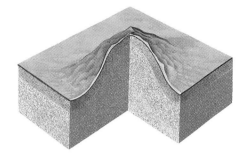

domesticated (dō mes'ti kāt əd) Tamed and/or bred to serve people's purposes. (D70) People breed *domesticated* animals such as horses for transportation and other uses.

dominant gene (däm'ə nənt jēn) A gene that has control over how a trait is expressed. (G14) A *dominant gene* will be expressed when paired with a recessive gene.

dominant trait (däm'ə nənt trāt) A trait that if inherited, will be expressed. (D45) Gregor Mendel found that tallness was a *dominant trait* in pea plants.

drag A force that resists forward motion through a fluid; it operates in the direction opposite to thrust. (F111) The air causes *drag* on an airplane.

earthquake A shaking or movement of Earth's surface, caused by the release of stored energy along a fault. (B58) Many *earthquakes* occur near the boundaries between tectonic plates.

egg A female sex cell. (G9) In sexual reproduction an *egg* is fertilized by a sperm.

electron (ē lek'trän) A negatively charged particle in an atom. (C71) The number of *electrons* in an atom usually equals the number of protons.

element (el'ə mənt) A substance that cannot be broken down into any other substance by ordinary chemical means. (C34) Oxygen, hydrogen, copper, iron, and carbon are *elements.*

embryo (em'brē ō) An early stage in the development of an organism. (G10) A fertilized egg develops into an *embryo.*

endangered species A species of animal or plant whose number has become so small that the species is in danger of becoming extinct. (D25) The rhinoceros has become an *endangered species* because poachers slaughter the animals for their horns.

endocrine gland (en'dō krin gland) A gland that produces hormones and releases them directly into the bloodstream. (G22) The thyroid and the pituitary are *endocrine glands.*

environmental risk factor A health risk factor that results from a person's environment. (G53) Breathing smoke from other people's cigarettes is an *environmental risk factor.*

epicenter (ep'i sent ər) The point on Earth's surface directly above an earthquake's point of origin. (B65) The *epicenter* of the earthquake was 2 km north of the city.

era (er'ə) One of the major divisions of geologic time. (D59) Many kinds of mammals developed during the Cenozoic *Era.*

ethanol (eth'ə nôl) A kind of alcohol used to make medicines, food products, and various other items. (A42) *Ethanol* is a flammable liquid.

evaporation (ē vap ə rā'shən) The change of state from a liquid to a gas. (C27) Heat from the Sun caused the *evaporation* of the water.

evolution (ev ə lo͞o'shən) The idea that all living things are descended from earlier forms of life, with new species developing over time. (D58) According to the theory of *evolution,* the plants and animals alive today descended from organisms that lived millions of years ago.

extinct (ek stiŋkt') With reference to species, no longer in existence. (D25) Dinosaurs are *extinct.*

extinction (ek stiŋk'shən) The disappearance of species from Earth. (D62) Scientists do not agree about what caused the *extinction* of the dinosaurs.

F

---

fault A break in rock along which rock slabs have moved. (B65) The shifting of Earth's tectonic plates can produce a *fault,* along which earthquakes may occur.

fault-block mountain A mountain formed when masses of rock move up or down along a fault. (B47) Mountains in the Great Rift Valley of Africa are *fault-block mountains.*

fermentation (fur mən tā'shən) A chemical change in which an organism breaks down sugar to produce carbon dioxide and alcohol or lactic acid. (A19, A42) The chemist used yeast to cause *fermentation* in the sugary liquid.

fertilization (fur tə li zā'shən) The process by which a sperm and an egg unite to form a cell that will develop into a new individual. (D24, G9) In humans, *fertilization* produces a cell containing 46 chromosomes, half from the female and half from the male.

fetus (fēt′əs) A stage in the development of an organism that follows the embryo stage. (G10) After about eight weeks, a human embryo is called a *fetus*.

first law of motion The concept that objects at rest tend to remain at rest and objects in motion tend to remain in motion, traveling at a constant speed and in the same direction. (F59) According to the *first law of motion*, a stationary object will stay in place unless some force makes it move.

fission (fish′ən) A method of asexual reproduction in which a parent cell divides to form two new cells. (A51, D10) Many one-celled organisms, such as amoebas, reproduce by *fission*.

focus (fō′kəs) The point, or place, at which an earthquake begins. (B65) The *focus* of the earthquake was about 20 km beneath Earth's surface.

folded mountain A mountain formed when two tectonic plates collide. (B45) The Alps and the Himalayas are *folded mountains*.

food pyramid A model showing the relative amounts of different kinds of food a person should eat each day for a healthful diet. (G59) Grains, including breads, cereals, rice, and pasta, make up the base of the *food pyramid*.

force A push or a pull. (F33, F65) The *force* of friction caused the rolling wagon to slow and then stop.

fossil (fäs′əl) The remains or traces of a living thing, usually preserved in rock. (D56) *Fossils* are usually found in sedimentary rock.

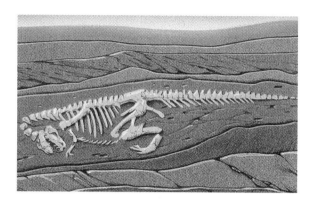

freezing The change of state from a liquid to a solid. (C28) The *freezing* of water occurs at 0°C.

friction (frik′shən) The rubbing of one thing against another. The force of friction resists motion between two surfaces that are in contact with each other. (F73) *Friction* keeps a car's tires from slipping off the road.

fungus (fuŋ′gəs) Any of a large group of organisms that feed on dead organisms or that are parasitic. (A43, G40) A mushroom is a *fungus*.

gene (jēn) One of the units that make up a chromosome; genes determine the traits an offspring inherits from its parent or parents. (D35, G13) Half of your *genes* come from your mother, and half come from your father.

gene splicing (jēn splīs′iŋ) A process by which genes are manipulated to alter the function or nature of an organism, usually by being transferred from one organism to another. (D48) Through *gene splicing*, scientists have transferred a gene for making insulin from one organism to another.

genetic engineering (jə net′ik en jə-nir′iŋ) The process by which genes are manipulated to bring about biological change in species. (D47) Using *genetic engineering* techniques, scientists have successfully combined DNA from different organisms.

gravity (grav′i tē) The force that pulls objects toward Earth; also, the attractive force exerted by a body or object on other bodies or objects. (F33) *Gravity* causes a ball to fall to the ground after it is thrown into the air.

health risk factor An action or condition that increases the probability of getting a disease or becoming injured. (G52) Smoking cigarettes and living in an area with severe water pollution are two *health risk factors.*

heat Energy that flows from warmer to cooler regions of matter. (C26) *Heat* can cause matter to change from one state to another.

hereditary risk factor A health risk factor that is passed on through genes from parent to child. (G52) A family history of heart disease is a *hereditary risk factor.*

hormone (hôr′mōn) A chemical substance that acts as a messenger, causing a change in organs and tissues in the body. (G23) Growth *hormones* are released by the pituitary gland.

hot spot A place deep within Earth's mantle that is extremely hot and contains a chamber of magma. (B102) Magma rising from a *hot spot* can break through Earth's crust to form a volcano.

immune system (im myo͞on′ sis′təm) The body's system that defends the body against pathogens. (A59, G33) The *immune system* produces antibodies to fight disease.

immunity (im myo͞on′i tē) The body's resistance to a disease or infection. (G35) Polio vaccine gives people *immunity* to the disease.

incomplete dominance (in kəm-plēt′ däm′ə nəns) The expression of both genes (traits) in a pair, producing a blended effect. (D46) A plant with pink flowers, produced by crossing a plant having red flowers with a plant having white flowers, is an example of *incomplete dominance.*

indicator (in'di kāt ər) A substance that changes color when mixed with an acid or a base. (C81) Paper treated with an *indicator* is used to test whether a compound is an acid or a base.

inertia (in ur'shə) The tendency of matter to remain at rest if at rest, or if in motion, to remain in motion in the same direction. (F59) *Inertia* results in passengers in a car moving forward when the driver applies the brakes.

inflammation (in flə mā'shən) A defense response by a part of the body, resulting from infection, injury, or irritation and marked by such symptoms as redness, pain, and swelling. (G33) The boy developed an *inflammation* where he had scraped his knee.

inherited trait (in her'it əd trāt) A trait that is passed on from parents to offspring by means of genes. (D34) Eye color is an *inherited trait*.

ion (ī'ən) An electrically charged atom. Ions form when atoms lose or gain electrons. (C73) A negative *ion* is formed when an atom gains electrons.

island arc A chain of volcanoes formed from magma that rises as a result of an oceanic plate sinking into the mantle. (B96) The Philippine Islands are part of an *island arc*.

K

kinetic energy (ki net'ik en'ər jē) Energy of motion. (C25) A ball rolling down a hill has *kinetic energy*.

L

lava (lä'və) Magma that flows out onto Earth's surface from a volcano. (B86) Flaming *lava* poured down the sides of the volcanic mountain.

law of conservation of mass The principle that states that matter can neither be created nor destroyed by a chemical or physical change. (C75) According to the *law of conservation of mass*, burning a log will not destroy any of the log's original mass.

law of conservation of momentum The principle that states that momentum can be transferred but cannot be lost. (F86) The *law of conservation of momentum* explains why the momentum resulting from the collision of two objects equals the total momentum of the objects before they collided.

learned trait (lʉrnd trāt) A trait that is acquired through learning or experience. (D36) The ability to speak Spanish is a *learned trait.*

lift The upward force, resulting from differences in air pressure above and below an airplane's wings, that causes the airplane to rise. (F111) Increasing the size of an airplane's wings increases *lift.*

lithosphere (lith'ō sfir) The solid, rocky layer of Earth, including the crust and top part of the mantle. (B38) The *lithosphere* is about 100 km thick.

magma (mag'mə) The hot, molten rock deep inside Earth. (B86) The *magma* rose through the volcano.

magnetic field (mag net'ik fēld) The space around a magnet within which the force of the magnet is exerted. (B28) The magnet attracted all the iron filings within its *magnetic field.*

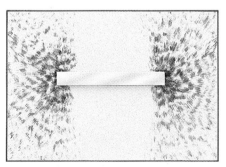

magnetic reversal (mag net'ik ri-vʉr'səl) The switching or changing of Earth's magnetic poles such that the north magnetic pole becomes located at the south magnetic pole's position and vice versa. (B28) Scientists have found evidence of *magnetic reversals* in layers of rock along the ocean floor.

magnitude (mag'nə tōōd) The force or strength of an earthquake. (B59) *Magnitude* is a measure of the amount of energy released by an earthquake.

mantle The middle layer of Earth. (B19) The *mantle* is the thick layer of rock between the crust and the core.

mass The amount of matter in an object. (C10, F33) A large rock has more *mass* than a pebble.

matter Anything that has mass and takes up space. (C10) Rocks, water, and air are three kinds of *matter.*

meiosis (mī ō'sis) The process of cell division by which the number of chromosomes in sex cells is reduced to half the number in body cells. (D22) Because of *meiosis*, a sex cell in a human has only 23 chromosomes instead of 46.

melting The change of state from a solid to a liquid. (C27) The *melting* of the icicles began after sunrise.

menstrual cycle (men'strəl sī'kəl) A cycle of approximately 28 days during which an egg is released by the ovary and, if not fertilized, leaves the body with other tissue and blood. (G24) The *menstrual cycle* begins when a girl reaches puberty.

metric system A system of measurement based on a few defined units (such as the meter) and in which larger and smaller units are related by powers of 10. (F11) In the *metric system*, a centimeter is 10 times longer than a millimeter.

microorganism (mī krō ôr'gən iz-əm) An organism too small to be seen except with the aid of a microscope. (G40) Bacteria are *microorganisms.*

mid-ocean ridge A chain of mountains under the ocean. (B22, E34) The *mid-ocean ridge* extends almost 60,000 km.

mitochondria (mīt ō kän'drē ə) Cell organelles in which energy is released from food. (A11) The more *mitochondria* a cell has, the more energy it can release from food.

mitosis (mī tō'sis) The process in which one cell divides to form two identical new cells. (A23) The new cells formed by *mitosis* have the same number of chromosomes as the parent cell.

mixture A combination of two or more substances that can be separated by physical means. (C34) This jar contains a *mixture* of colored beads.

model Something used or made to represent an object or an idea. (C71) The plastic *model* showed the structure of the heart.

mold fossil (mōld fäs'əl) A fossil consisting of a hollowed space in the shape of an organism or one of its parts. (D56) Sediments collecting around a dead organism may lead to the formation of a *mold fossil* of the organism.

molecule (mäl'i kyōōl) A particle made up of a group of atoms that are chemically bonded. (C39) A *molecule* of water contains three atoms.

momentum (mō men'təm) A property of a moving object, calculated by multiplying the object's mass by its velocity. (F85) The train gathered *momentum* as its speed increased.

moneran (män'ər an) Any of mostly one-celled organisms in which the cell does not have a nucleus. (A50) Bacteria are *monerans.*

mucus (myōō'kəs) A thick, sticky fluid that lines the membranes of the respiratory system. (G33) *Mucus* helps trap particles that you breathe in.

multicellular (mul ti sel'yōō lər) Made up of more than one cell. (A33) Some protists are *multicellular.*

mutation (myo͞o tā′shən) A change in a gene that can result in a new characteristic, or trait. (D76) Certain *mutations* have helped species survive in their environment.

natural selection (nach′ər əl sə-lek′shən) The process by which those living things that have characteristics adapting them to their environment tend to live longest and produce the most offspring, passing on these favorable characteristics to their offspring. (D75) *Natural selection* helps explain why certain characteristics become common while others die out.

neap tide (nēp tīd) The tide occurring at the first and third quarters of the Moon, when the difference in level between high and low tide is smallest. (E71) *Neap tides* occur at two times during a month.

nekton (nek′tän) All the free-swimming animals that live in the ocean. (E25) *Nekton* include such animals as fish, octopuses, and whales.

neutralization (no͞o trəl ī zā′shən) The reaction between an acid and a base. (C83) *Neutralization* produces water and a salt.

neutron (no͞o′trän) A particle in the nucleus of an atom that has no electric charge. (C71) The mass of a *neutron* is about equal to that of a proton.

newton (no͞o′tən) A unit used to measure force. (F66) A *newton* is the force needed to accelerate a one-kilogram object by one meter per second every second.

nuclear fission (no͞o′klē ər fish′ən) The splitting of the nucleus of an atom, releasing great amounts of energy. (C77) Bombarding a nucleus with a neutron can cause *nuclear fission*.

nuclear membrane The structure that surrounds and encloses the nucleus and controls what substances move into and out of the nucleus. (A11) The *nuclear membrane* appears to be solid, but it actually has tiny holes through which materials can pass.

nucleus (no͞o′klē əs) 1. The dense, central part of an atom. (C71) The *nucleus* contains nearly all of an atom's mass. 2. The control center of a cell. (A11) The *nucleus* contains the cell's genetic information.

obese (ō bēs′) More than 20 percent over normal body weight. (G60) *Obese* people have more health problems than people of normal weight.

organ A part of an multicellular organism made up of a group of tissues that work together to perform a certain function. (A26) The heart and the lungs are *organs* of the human body.

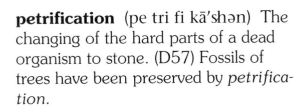

organ system A group of organs that work together to perform one or more functions. (A26) The stomach and the intestines are part of the *organ system* that digests food.

osmosis (äs mō′sis) The diffusion of water through a membrane. (A16) *Osmosis* maintains the balance of water inside and outside a cell.

— P —

paleontologist) (pā lē ən täl′ə jist) A scientist who studies fossils. (D58) A team of *paleontologists* discovered the remains of a dinosaur.

Pangaea (pan jē′ə) A supercontinent that existed about 200 million years ago. (B9) *Pangaea* broke apart into several continents.

pathogen (path′ə jən) A microorganism that can cause a disease. (G40) A virus is a *pathogen.*

period 1. A division of geologic time that is a subdivision of an era. (D59) The Jurassic *Period* is part of the Mesozoic Era. 2. The interval of time between two successive wave crests. (E65) The *period* for the ocean waves was about ten seconds.

petrification (pe tri fi kā′shən) The changing of the hard parts of a dead organism to stone. (D57) Fossils of trees have been preserved by *petrification.*

photosynthesis (fōt ō sin′thə sis) The process by which green plants and other producers use light energy to make food. (A18, E24) In *photosynthesis,* plant cells use light energy to make glucose from carbon dioxide and water.

physical change A change in size, shape, or state of matter, with no new kind of matter being formed. (C68) The freezing of water into ice cubes is an example of a *physical change.*

physical properties (fiz′i kəl präp′ər tēz) Characteristics of matter that can be measured or detected by the senses. (C34) Color is a *physical property* of minerals.

phytoplankton (fīt ō plaŋk′tən) Any of the usually microscopic plantlike protists that live near the surface of the ocean. (E11) *Phytoplankton* drift with the ocean currents.

plankton (plaŋk′tən) Organisms, generally microscopic in size, that float or drift in the ocean. (A35, E11) *Plankton* is a source of food for fish.

plate One of the slabs that make up Earth's crust and upper mantle; also called *tectonic plate.* (B19) Some of Earth's *plates* carry continents.

plate boundary A place where the plates that make up Earth's crust and upper mantle either move together or apart or else move past one another. (B20, B40) Earthquakes occur along *plate boundaries*.

pollution The contamination of the environment with waste materials or other unwanted substances. (E91) Dangerous chemicals dumped into the ocean are one source of *pollution*.

polymer (päl'ə mər) A compound consisting of large molecules formed from many smaller, linked molecules. (C92) Proteins are *polymers*.

protist (prōt'ist) Any of a large group of mostly single-celled, microscopic organisms. (A33) Amoebas and algae are *protists*.

proton (prō'tän) A positively charged particle found in the nucleus of an atom. (C71) The atomic number of an atom equals the number of *protons* in the atom's nucleus.

protozoan (prō tō zō'ən) Protists that have animal-like traits. (A34, G40) A paramecium is a *protozoan*.

puberty (pyo͞o'bər tē) The state of physical development when a person becomes capable of producing offspring. (G22) Girls generally reach *puberty* earlier than boys.

radioactive element (rā dē ō ak'tiv el'ə mənt) An element made up of atoms whose nuclei break down, or decay, into nuclei of other atoms. (C76) As the nucleus of a *radioactive element* decays, energy is released.

reaction force The force exerted in response to an action force. (F92) A *reaction force* is equal in strength to an action force but opposite in direction.

recessive gene (ri ses'iv jēn) A gene that is able to control how a trait is expressed only when paired with another recessive gene. (G14) A *recessive gene* will not be expressed when paired with a dominant gene.

recessive trait (ri ses'iv trāt) A trait that will be hidden if paired with a dominant trait. (D45) In his experiments with pea plants, Gregor Mendel learned that shortness was a *recessive trait*.

reproduction The process by which organisms produce more of their own kind. (D10) *Reproduction* ensures the survival of the species.

Richter scale (rik'tər skāl) A scale of numbers by which the magnitude of earthquakes is measured. (B59) Each increase of 1.0 on the *Richter scale* represents an increase of 30 times in the energy released by an earthquake.

rifting (rift′iŋ) The process by which magma rises to fill the gap between two plates that are moving apart. (B108) *Rifting* in eastern Africa may split the continent into two parts.

salinity (sə lin′ə tē) The total amount of dissolved salts in ocean water. (E9) The *salinity* of the ocean varies in different parts of the world.

salt A compound that can be formed when an acid reacts with a base. (C83) When vinegar and baking soda interact, they produce a *salt*.

saprophyte (sap′rə fīt) An organism that lives on dead or decaying matter. (A44) Molds are *saprophytes*.

sea-floor spreading The process by which new ocean floor is continually being formed as magma rises to the surface and hardens into rock. (B30) *Sea-floor spreading* occurs as magma fills the space between separating plates.

seamount (sē′mount) An underwater mountain that formed from a volcano. (E34) Thousands of *seamounts* rise from the floor of the Pacific.

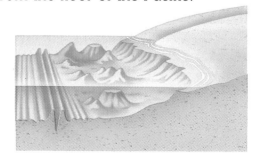

second law of motion The concept that an object's acceleration is related to the strength of the force acting on it and on the object's mass. (F65) A gust of wind blowing an open umbrella out of your hands illustrates the *second law of motion*.

seismograph (sīz′mə graf) An instrument that records the intensity, duration, and nature of earthquake waves. (B74) Scientists use information from *seismographs* to determine the location of earthquakes.

seismometer (sīz mäm′ə tər) An instrument that detects and records Earth's movements. (B98) Data from the *seismometer* suggested that a volcanic eruption might soon occur.

selective breeding Breeding of living things to produce offspring with certain desired characteristics. (D70) People have used *selective breeding* to produce domesticated animals.

sex cell A female or male reproductive cell; an egg cell or sperm cell. (D22) Reproduction can occur when *sex cells* unite.

sexual reproduction Reproduction that involves the joining of a male sex cell and a female sex cell. (D22, G9) Most animals and plants produce offspring through *sexual reproduction*.

shield volcano A kind of volcano that is large and gently sloped and that is formed when lava flows quietly from a crack in the Earth's crust. (B89) Mauna Loa, a *shield volcano* in Hawaii, is the largest volcano on Earth.

solute (säl'yo͞ot) The material present in the smaller amount in a solution; the substance dissolved in a solution. (C57) If you dissolve sugar in water, sugar is the *solute*.

solution A mixture in which the different particles are spread evenly throughout the mixture. (C57) Dissolving salt in water makes a *solution*.

solvent (säl'vənt) The material present in the greater amount in a solution; the substance in a solution, usually a liquid, that dissolves another substance. (C57) If you mix sugar and water, water is the *solvent*.

speed The distance traveled in a certain amount of time; rate of movement. (F16) The truck was moving at a *speed* of 40 mph.

sperm (spurm) A male sex cell. (G9) A *sperm* combines with an egg during fertilization.

spore A reproductive cell that can develop into a new organism. (A43) Ferns and mushrooms produce *spores*.

spring tide A tide occurring at or just after the new moon and full moon; usually the highest tide of the month. (E71) At the time of a *spring tide*, both the Sun and the Moon are in line with Earth.

state of matter Any of the three forms that matter may take: solid, liquid, or gas. (C20) Water's *state of matter* depends on its temperature.

substance Matter of a particular kind, or chemical makeup. (C34) Elements and compounds are *substances*.

symbiosis (sim bī ō'sis) A relationship between two organisms in which at least one organism benefits. (A61) Some fungi and algae grow together in *symbiosis*.

tectonic plate See plate.

temperature A measure of the average kinetic energy of the particles in matter. (C26) Water *temperature* rises as the motion of water molecules increases.

theory of continental drift A theory that states that the continents formed a single land mass at one time in the past and have drifted over time to their present positions. (B10) The idea of *continental drift* was first suggested by Alfred Wegener.

theory of plate tectonics The theory that Earth's lithosphere is broken into enormous slabs, or plates, that are in motion. (B19, B41) Scientists use the *theory of plate tectonics* to explain how Earth's continents drift.

third law of motion The concept that for every action force there is an equal and opposite reaction force. (F92) When you watch someone's feet bouncing off a trampoline, you see the *third law of motion* at work.

thrust (thrust) The push or driving force that causes an airplane, rocket, or other object to move forward. (F110) *Thrust* can be produced by a spinning propeller or by a jet engine.

tide The daily rise and fall of the surface of the ocean or other large body of water, caused by the gravitational attraction of the Moon and the Sun. (E70) As the *tide* came in, we moved our blanket back from the water's edge.

tissue A group of similar, specialized cells working together to carry out the same function. (A25) Muscle *tissue* contains cells that contract.

toxin (täks'in) A poison produced by an organism. (A58) *Toxins* produced by bacteria can cause serious illness.

trade wind A prevailing wind that blows from east to west on either side of the equator. (E56) South of the equator, the *trade wind* comes from the southeast.

transform-fault boundary (transfôrm fôlt boun'də rē) A place where the plates that make up Earth's crust and upper mantle move past one another. (B41) Movement occurring at a *transform-fault boundary* may cause cracks to form in Earth's rocks.

tsunami (tsoo nä'mē) A large and powerful ocean wave usually caused by an underwater earthquake. (B76) A *tsunami* can cause great destruction if it strikes a land area.

turbidity current (tᵤr bid'i tē kᵤr'ənt) A current of water carrying large amounts of sediment. (E38, E61) *Turbidity currents* may cause sediment to build up in some places.

upper mantle (up'ər man'təl) The outermost part of the mantle. (B20) Earth's plates consist of a thin layer of crust lying over the *upper mantle.*

upwelling The rising of deep water to the surface that occurs when winds move surface water. (E60) *Upwelling* brings pieces of shells and dead organisms up from the ocean floor.

vaccine (vak sēn′) A preparation of dead or weakened bacteria or viruses that produces immunity to a disease. (A59, G35) The *vaccine* for smallpox has eliminated that disease.

vacuole (vak′yo͞o ōl) A structure in the cytoplasm in which food and other substances are stored. (A11) A *vacuole* in a plant cell is often quite large.

vegetative propagation (vej ə tāt′iv präp ə gā′shən) A form of asexual reproduction in which a new plant develops from a part of a parent plant. (D15) Using a cutting taken from a houseplant to grow a new plant is a method of *vegetative propagation.*

velocity (və läs′ə tē) The rate of motion in a particular direction. (F21) The *velocity* was northwest at 880 km/h.

virus (vī′rəs) A tiny disease-causing life form consisting of genetic material wrapped inside a capsule of protein. (A52, G40) *Viruses* cause such diseases as AIDS, chickenpox, and rabies.

volcano An opening in Earth's crust through which hot gases, rock fragments, and molten rock erupt. (B48, B86) Lava flowed out of the *volcano.*

volume (väl′yo͞om) The amount of space that matter takes up. (C11) A large fuel tank holds a greater *volume* of gasoline than a small tank.

wave The up-and-down movement of the surface of water, caused by the wind. (E65) Ocean *waves* crashed against the shoreline.

wavelength The distance between the crests of two successive waves. (E65) At the height of the storm, the waves had a *wavelength* of 10 m.

weight A measure of the force of gravity on an object. (F33) The *weight* of this package is five pounds.

westerly (wes′tər lē) A prevailing wind that blows from west to east. (E56) Ships that sailed from North America to Europe were aided by the power of the *westerlies.*

zooplankton (zō ō plaŋk′tən) Any of the tiny animal-like organisms that live near the surface of the ocean. (E11) Zooplankton float in the sea.

zygote (zī′gōt) A fertilized egg cell. (D24, G10) A zygote develops into an embryo by means of cell division.

INDEX

*Activity

* **Activity**

*Activity

CREDITS

Cover: *Design, Art Direction, and Production:* Design Five, NYC; *Photography:* Jade Albert; *Photography Production:* Picture It Corporation; *Illustration:* Marti Shohet. **TOC:** Terry Boles, Barbara Cousins, Bob Radigan, Nadine Sokol, John Youssi.

ILLUSTRATORS

UNIT 6A Opener: Lane Yerkes. **Chapter A1:** Keith Kasnot: 22, 23; Briar Lee Mitchell: 26; Michael Kress-Russick: 17, 26; Teri McDermott: 10, 11; Walter Stuart: 25; Ray Vella: 18, 19. **Chapter A2:** David Flaherty: 43, 44; Virge Kask: 33; Kirk Moldoff: 37; Yvonne Walston: 39; Lane Yerkes: 28, 29. **Chapter A3:** Barbara Cousins: 50, 51, 53; Eldon Doty: 55; Ken Tiessen: 61, 62.

UNIT 6B Chapter B1: Skip Baker: 22; Dolores Bego: 7, 30; Warren Budd: 19, 20, 31; Eldon Doty: 8, 9; Eureka Cartography: 17, 18, 20, 21; Geo Systems: 12, 13, 14, 15; Dale Glasgow & Assoc.: 10; Brad Gaber: 29; Greg Harris: 26, 27; Bill Morris: 28; Claudia Karabaic Sargent: 11; Ray Smith: 12, 13, 14, 15. **Chapter B2:** Julie Carpenter: 40, 41; Brad Gaber: 38, 39, 40, 41; Eureka Cartography: 41, 43, 51; Ben Perini 49; Bob Swanson: 45, 47, 48; Randy Verougstraete: 49. **Chapter B3:** Dolores Bego: 77; Bob Brugger: 64; Julie Carpenter: 76, 77, 78; Eldon Doty: 56, 57; Eureka Cartography: 55, 59; Patrick Gnan: 79, 80; Greg Harris: 76, 77, 102; Robert Roper: 64, 65, 67, 81; Robert Schuster: 60; Joe Spencer: 75. **Chapter B4:** Stephen Baur: 107; Dolores Bego: 87; Eldon Doty: 93; Eureka Cartography: 90, 101, 102, 110; Dale Glasgow & Assoc.: 105; Greg Harris: 102, 103, 111; Susan Johnson Carlson: 110; Laszlo Kubini: 92, 96; Bob Swanson: 86, 96, 97; John Youssi: 88, 89, 108, 109.

UNIT 6C Chapter C1: Terry Boles: 15; Patrick Gnan: 11; Mark McIntosh: 29; Andy Meyer: 10, 11, 12; Robert Pasternack: 26, 27; Scott Ross: 12, 19, 20, 21. **Chapter C2:** Bob Brugger: 51; Bill Fox: 34; Adam Mathews: 58; Bob Radigan: 57; Nadine Sokol: 39, 40, 41; Paul Woods: 36, 37, 61. **Chapter C3:** Eldon Doty: 75; Patrick Gnan: 69, 90; George Hardebeck: 76; Steven Mach: 82, 83; Ken Rosenborg: 76, 77; Robert Schuster: 92, 94; Nadine Sokol: 70, 72, 73, 74.

UNIT 6D Chapter D1: Karl Edwards: 10, 11, 12; J.A.K. Graphics: 19, 21, 23; Nina Laden: 10, 11; Kirk Moldoff: 24; Wendy Smith-Griswold: 15, 16, 17. **Chapter D2:** Barbara Cousins: 38, 40, 45; Terry Kovalcik: 37; Sudi McCollum: 33; Teri McDermott: 34, 35, 36, 37, 47; Marjorie Muns: 44, 45; Linda Nye: 42. **Chapter D3:** Drew Brook Cormack: 68, 69; Mona Conner: 74, 75, 76; Richard Courtney: 62; Andy Lendway: 59, 79; Christine Schaar: 66, 67; Raymond Smith: 59, 60, 61; David Uhl: 56, 57; Rosemary Volpe: 70.

UNIT 6E Chapter E1: Terry Boles: 17; Adam Mathews: 17; Bob Radigan: 8, 9, 10, 11; Jim Salvati: 24, 25; Robert Schuster: 11. **Chapter E2:** Barbara Hoopes Ambler: 43; Adam Mathews: 38; Joe McDermott: 32, 33, 49; Steven Nau: 36, 37, 38, 39; Jon Prud' Homme: 36; Bob Radigan: 44, 45; Jeff Seaver: 39. **Chapter E3:** Greg Harris: 65, 73; Jeffery Hitch: 56, 59; Catherine Leary: 65, 66; Adam Mathews: 58, 59, 60, 61; Steven Nau: 62, 63; Jon Prud' Homme: 70, 71; Peter Spacek: 55, 56, 57; Bob Radigan: 92, 93; Gary Torrisi: 84, 85. **Chapter E4:** Eldon Doty: 82, 83; Bob Radigan: E92, E93; Michael Sloan: 80; Dean St. Clair: 91, 92, 93, 94, 95; Gary Torrisi: 84, 85, 86.

UNIT 6F Opener: Ron Fleming **Chapter F1:** Terry Boles: 8, 9, 10; Art Cumings: 24; David Klug: 26; A. J. Miller: 14; Jeffrey Oh: 16, 17; Linda Richards: 25. **Chapter F2:** Terry Boles: 32, 33, 35; Eldon Doty: 38; Don Dixon: 47; Larry Jost: 48, 49; Rebecca Merrilees: 43; Lois Leonard Stock: 46, 47. **Chapter F3:** Terry Boles: 65; Ron Fleming: 52, 53; Dale Glasgow & Assoc.: 68, 69, 77; Jeffery Lynch: 60, 61; Linda Richards: 73, 74, 75, 76; Scott Ross: 58, 59; Michael Sloan: 55, 56, 57. **Chapter F4:** Larry Jost: 95; Bob Novak: 93; Sergio Roffo: 84; Ron Young: 82, 83. **Chapter F5:** Terry Boles: 106, 107, 117; Julie Carpenter: 109; Bob Novak 110, 111, 124; Pete Spacek: 123, 124, 125, 126.

UNIT 6G Opener: Iskra Johnson. **Chapter G1:** Anatoly Chernistov: 22, 23; Iskra Johnson: 4, 5; Claude Martinot: 12, 13, 14, 15; Briar Lee Mitchell: 7; Mary Ellen Niates: 9, 10, 11, 17; Julie Peterson: 25, 26; Stephen Schudlich: 9, 10, 11, 16; Matt Straub: 20, 21; Kate Sweeney: 13, 14, 27. **Chapter G2:** Barbara Cousins: 40, 41; David Flaherty: 32; Marcia Hartsock: 46; Jackie Heda: 32, 33, 34, 35, 47; Briar Lee Mitchell: 42, 43; Leonid Mysakov: 36. **Chapter G3:** Mark Bender: 51, 52, 53; Glasgow & Assoc.: 57; Steven Stankiewicz: 54, 55; Rod Thomas: 59, 60, 61, 62, 63; Beth Anne Willert: 61.

Glossary: Warren Budd and Assoc., Barbara Cousins, Brad Gaber, Patrick Gnan, Verlin Miller, Bob Swanson, David Uhl, John Youssi.

Handbook: Kathleen Dunne, Laurie Hamilton, Catherine Leary, Andy Meyer

Unit A Opener 1–3: © M.I. Walker/Science Source/Photo Researchers. 2: *l.* Grant Heilman Photography. **Chapter 1** 4–5: *bkgd.* David M. Phillips/Visuals Unlimited; *inset* Richard Hutchings for SBG. 6: Ken Karp for SBG. 7: *t.* Ken Karp for SBG; *b.l.* Ken Karp for SBG; *b.r.* © Nursidsany et Perennou/Photo Researchers, Inc. 8: Ken Karp for SBG. 10: © Biophoto Associates/Science Source/Photo Researchers, Inc. 12: *t.* The Science Museum, London/Science & Society Picture Library; *b.* The Science Museum/Science & Society Picture Library. 13: *b.* © Photo Researchers, Inc. 14–16: Ken Karp for SBG. 18: Ruth Dixon/Stock Boston. 19: PhotoEdit. 20: Ken Karp for SBG. 21: Carolina

Biological/Phototake. 22: *l.* © M. Abbey/Photo Researchers, Inc.; *m.* © M. Abbey/Photo Researchers, Inc.; *r.* © M. Abbey/Photo Researchers, Inc. 23: *l.* © M. Abbey/Photo Researchers, Inc.; *r.* © M. Abbey/Photo Researchers, Inc. 24: Merritt A. Vincent/Photo Edit. 25: David Dennis/Tom Stack & Associates. 26: *t.m.* John Cunningham/Visuals Unlimited; *b.* Cabisco/Visuals Unlimited. **Chapter 2** 28: S. Rannels/Grant Heilman Photography. 30: *t.* Carolina Biological Supply Co.; *b.l.* © Photo Researchers, Inc.; *b.r.* © M.I. Walker/Photo Researchers, Inc. 31: *b.* Carolina Biological Supply/Custom Medical Stock. 32: *b.* Bruce Iverson. 33: *t.* J. Robert Waaland/Biological Photo Service; *b.* Alfred Owczarzak/Biological Photo Service. 34: *t.l.* © Photo Researchers, Inc.; *t.r.* Custom Medical Stock; *b.* Manfred Kage/Peter Arnold. 35: *t.l.* © Nuridsany et Pereennou/Photo Researchers, Inc.; *t.m.l.* © Walker/Photo Researchers, Inc.; *t.m.r.* Roger Klocek/Visuals Unlimited; *t.r.* © Photo Researchers, Inc.; *m.* Manfred Kage/Peter Arnold; *b.* Carolina Biological/Phototake. 36: © M.I. Walker/Photo Researchers, Inc. 38: E. R. Degginger/Color-Pics, Inc. 41: *r.* © Photo Researchers, Inc. 43: *b.* Carolina Biological Supply Co. 44: *t.* © Sidney Moulds/Photo Researchers, Inc.; *b.l.* E. R. Degginger/Color-Pics, Inc.; *b.r.* Sherman Thomson/Visuals Unlimited. **Chapter 3** 46: *bkgd.* Institut Pasteur/CNRI/Phototake. 47: *inset* Ian Howarth. 51: E. R. Degginger/Color-Pics, Inc.; 52: J.L. Carson/Custom Medical Stock. 53: © Biophoto Association/Photo Researchers, Inc.; 54–55: The Bettmann Archive. AP/Wide World Photos; *m.r.* Sipa Press; *b.l.* The Bettmann Archive; *b.m.* The Schomberg Collection/The New York Public Library; *b.r.* Sipa Press. 59: J. L. Carson/Custom Medical Stock. 60: Kevin Walsh/UCSD. 61: © Photo Researchers, Inc. 62: *l.* © Will & Deni McIntyre/Photo Researchers, Inc; 2: © Stephen J. Kraseman/Photo Researchers, Inc.

Unit B Opener: Liaison International. 2: Peter French. **Chapter 1** 4: *inset* © Tom Van Sant/Geosphere Project, Santa Monica/Photo Researchers, Inc. 4–5: *bkgd.* Richard Johnston/FPG International; 9: Courtesy, Dover Publications. 31: Bob Krist. **Chapter 2** 34: *r. inset* Lamont-Doherty Earth Observatory. 34.35: *bkgd.* Don Blankenship-UTIG; *l.inset* Jean Miele; *m. inset* Lawrence A. Lanver. 39: Phil Degginger/Color-Pics, Inc. 40: Bob Krist. 41: © David Parker/Science Photo Library/Photo Researchers, Inc. . 45: *r.* Superstock. 47: *t.* Dr. E. R. Degginger/Color-Pics, Inc.; *b* Rich Buzzelli/Tom Stack & Associates. 48: *t.* © Emil Muench/Photo Researchers, Inc.; *m.* Ralph Perry/Tony Stone Images; *b.* Larry Nielsen/Peter Arnold. 50: *l.* Superstock; *r.* AP/Wide World Photos. **Chapter 3** 52–53: *bkgd.* Les Stone/Sygma; *inset* Gaylon Wampler/Sygma. 56: *t.* The Bettmann Archive; *b.* The Granger Collection. 58: © Will and Deni McIntyre/Photo Researchers, Inc. 61: © David Parker/Science Photo Library/Photo Researchers, Inc. 62: AP/Wide World Photos. 67: Shahn Kermani/Liaison International. 72–73: Grant Huntington for SBG. 74: Michael Holford. 78: Ken Biggs/Tony Stone Images. 79: James Stanfield/ © National Geographic Society. 80: Mark Downey/Liaison International. **Chapter 4** 82–83: *bkgd.* Dean Conger/© National Geographic Society; *inset* © 1991 *Discover* Magazine. 87: *l.* Mikhail Zhilin/Bruce Coleman; *r.* Franco Salmoiraghi. 88: Robert Frerck/Odyssey Productions. 89: *t.* Tony Stone Images; *b.* Phil Degginger/Color-Pics, Inc. 90: *l.* Stella Snead/Bruce Coleman; *r.* K. Eriksson/Liaison International. 92: *l.* Scala/Art Resource; *r.* Alinari/Art Resource. 97: © Robert M. Carey/NOAA/Science Photo Library/Photo Researchers, Inc. 98: *t.* AP/Wide World Photos; *b.* AP/Wide World Photos. 99: Peter French. 103: Werner Forman Archive/British Museum/Art Resource. 104: *t.* Dr. Alexander Malahoff/HURL; *b.* James Cachero/Sygma. 106: NASA. 109: Rick Carson/Liaison International.

Unit C Opener: 1–3: ©William McCoy/Rainbow. 2: David Young–Wolff/PhotoEdit. **Chapter 1** 4: *bkgd.* Tom Bean/The Stock Market; *inset* David S. Hik/Nunatak International. 6–24: Richard Hutchings for SBG. 25: © Francois Gohier/Photo Researchers, Inc. 28: *l.* © Scott Camazine/Photo Researchers, Inc. **Chapter 2** 30: *bkgd.* Tom Stack & Associates; *inset* ESA/TSADO/Tom Stack & Associates. 32–35: Grant Huntington for SBG. 39–40: *l.* Yoav Levy/Phototake. 42: *l.* © George Holton/National Archaeological Museum/Photo Researchers, Inc.; *r.* Culver Pictures. 43: *t.b.* Culver Pictures 44–49: Grant Huntington for SBG. 50: *l.* Robert Yager/Tony Stone Images; *r.* Bill Ross/Tony Stone Images. 51: Steve Weinrebe/Stock Boston. 52–55: Grant Huntington for SBG. 56: NASA/Tom Stack & Associates. 57: *l.r.* Grant Huntington for SBG. 58: David Young–Wolff/PhotoEdit. 59: *t.* Ken Lax for SBG; *b.l., b.m., b.r.* Boltin Picture Library. **Chapter 3** 62: *bkgd.* Michael Fogden/DRK Photo; *inset* Steve Winter/Black Star. 65–68: *t.* Ken Karp for SBG. 69: *t.* D. Cavagnaro/DRK Photo; *m.* John Gerlach/DRK Photo. 74–75: The Bettman Archive. 78–82: Ken Karp for SBG. 84: Tom Stack & Associates. 85: © Jim Corwin/Photo Researchers, Inc. 86–92: Ken Karp for SBG. 93: Pat Lanza Field/Bruce Coleman. 95: E. R. Degginger/Color-Pics, Inc.; *r.* Phil Degginger/Color-Pics, Inc.

Unit D Opener: 1–3: Custom Medical Stock. 2: Hinterleitner/Gamma Liaison. **Chapter 1** 4: *bkgd.* Corey Meitchik/Custom Medical Stock ; *inset* Grace Moore/Morristown Memorial Hospital. 6: Grant Huntington for SBG. 7: © M. Abbey/Photo Researchers, Inc.; 8: Grant Huntington for SBG. 9: © Biophoto Associates/Photo Researchers, Inc. 11: Dwight R. Kuhn. 13: © Biophoto Associates/Photo Researchers, Inc.; *m.t. m. b.* © M. I. Walker/Photo Researchers, Inc. 14: William E. Ferguson; 15: *bkgd.* Lefever/Grushow/Grant Heilman Photography; *inset* Lefever/Grushow/Grant Heilman Photography. 16: *t.* Dwight R. Kuhn; *m.l.* Runk/Schoenberger/Grant Heilman Photography; *m.r.,b.* Grant Heilman Photography; 17: *l.* Larry Lefever/Grant Heilman Photography; *m.* Dwight R. Kuhn; *r.* The Granger Collection. 18–20: Grant Huntington for SBG. 22: © David M. Phillips/Photo Researchers, Inc. 25: *t.* E. R. Degginger/Color-Pics, Inc.; *b.* The Granger Collection. 26: *t.* Ron Garrison/Zoological Society of San Diego; *b.* Steve Kaufman/DRK Photo. 27: © M. Abbey/Photo Researchers, Inc. **Chapter 2** 28: *bkgd.* Dr. Jack Hearn/U.S. Department of Agricultural Research; *inset* Dr. Jack Hearn/U.S. Department of Agricultural Research. 30–35: Grant Huntington for SBG. 36: *l.* Focus on Sports; *m.* Michael Ponzini/Focus on Sports; *r.* Sports Chrome. 39–41: Grant Huntington for SBG. 44: Bill Horseman Photography/Stock Boston. 45: Austrian Institute. 46: Courtesy, Marcus Rhoades. 48: *l.* David M. Dennis/Tom Stack & Associates; *r.* Bob Daemmrich. **Chapter 3** 50: *bkgd.* Larry Dale Gordon/The Image Bank; *inset* Robert Maier/Animals Animals. 52: Ken Lax for SBG. 53: *t.* Ken Lax for SBG; *m.* Breck Kent/Earth Scenes; *b.l.* © James Amos/Photo Researchers, Inc.; *b.r.* Breck Kent/Earth Scenes. 54–55: Ken Lax for SBG. 57: *l.* © Eric Hosking/Photo Researchers, Inc.; *r.* Wendell Metzen/Bruce Coleman.